THE ANCIENT WALK-ABOUT WAY

The Divine Avataric Great Sage,
ADI DA SAMRAJ

THE ANCIENT WALK-ABOUT WAY

The Core Esoteric Process of Real Spirituality
and Its Perfect Fulfillment in the Way of Adidam

THE DIVINE AVATARIC GREAT SAGE,
ADI DA SAMRAJ

THE DAWN HORSE PRESS
MIDDLETOWN, CALIFORNIA

NOTE TO THE READER

All who study the Way of Adidam or take up its practice should remember that they are responding to a Call to become responsible for themselves. They should understand that they, not Avatar Adi Da Samraj or others, are responsible for any decision they make or action they take in the course of their lives of study or practice.

The devotional, Spiritual, functional, practical, relational, and cultural practices and disciplines referred to in this book are appropriate and natural practices that are voluntarily and progressively adopted by members of the practicing congregations of Adidam (as appropriate to the personal circumstance of each individual). Although anyone may find these practices useful and beneficial, they are not presented as advice or recommendations to the general reader or to anyone who is not a member of one of the practicing congregations of Adidam. And nothing in this book is intended as a diagnosis, prescription, or recommended treatment or cure for any specific "problem", whether medical, emotional, psychological, social, or Spiritual. One should apply a particular program of treatment, prevention, cure, or general health only in consultation with a licensed physician or other qualified professional.

The Ancient Walk-About Way is formally authorized for publication by the Ruchira Sannyasin Order of Adidam Ruchiradam. (The Ruchira Sannyasin Order of Adidam Ruchiradam is the senior Cultural Authority within the formal gathering of formally acknowledged devotees of the Avataric Great Sage, Adi Da Samraj.)

Produced by the Dawn Horse Press,
a division of the Avataric Pan-Communion of Adidam.

International Standard Book Number: 1-57097-221-4
Library of Congress Catalog Card Number: 2006938168

CONTENTS

The Unique Advantage for Humankind

An Introduction to
The Ancient Walk-About Way
by Megan Anderson

Since ancient times, human beings have desired Revelation of What is Greater than their daily experience of pain and pleasure, Greater than their "survival mode" disposition toward all that comes between birth and death. Some human ideas of a Great Reality are recorded in the histories and artifacts of civilization; some of them are perhaps lost forever, buried either by the earth itself, or by the twists of time and cultural habit. But again and again the core impulse of the human being has come to the fore, the search for a form in which to relate to the Great Mystery of existence.

From time to time, that longing has found expression in the direct human relationship with one who has actually—to whatever degree—<u>Realized</u> the Truth of existence, rather than just wondered about it. Where such exceptional beings have appeared, they have been noticed and praised, supplicated for wisdom, worshipped and cherished for the help they could offer in the process of seeking the Ultimate Truth.

The One Who Speaks to you in this book makes unnecessary any further human seeking of any kind. These essays are a celebration of Perfect Divine Revelation, founded in a unique and Absolute Knowledge of Reality Itself. The Appearance of Adi Da Samraj is the Direct Intervention of Truth in the world of appearances. Through His Divine and Avataric Incarnation, Adi Da Samraj Offers both the Unqualified Knowledge of Existence and the greatest Helping Means for such Knowledge to manifest.

The Great Tradition of the "Walk-About Way"

As the title of this book emphasizes, Adi Da's Offering stands in continuity with the root-essence of even the most ancient forms of human religion. That Way is the spontaneous, non-verbal response to the mere sight of an illumined being. Such responsive transformation is not bound by pre-conceived doctrine or formalized practice. This secret heart of true religion has existed since before the annals of human time, because it is intrinsic to the human being—not dependent on writing, institutions, or any of the hallmarks of "history" and "civilization".

Thus, the Wisdom-Way that Avatar Adi Da has Given is, in its fundamental practice, part of a Great Tradition—which began, with the earliest human beings, walking the Earth over fifty thousand years ago. According to genetic evidence, it was such wanderings that eventually produced all apparent variation of the human species.*[1] This is the sense in which Adi Da uses the term "Walk-About"[2]: the unity of humanity in intelligent association with its environment, not disconnected by the abstractions of mind, and thus free to directly respond to the Revelation of Truth wherever it is Given. As Adi Da Samraj once described to a gathering of His devotees:

Though there are many historical traditions of religion and Spirituality, in Truth, there is one Great Tradition. In fact, that Great Tradition is even older than the history that humankind has recorded. There is a prehistorical background to all the historical traditions—which I call a "Walk-About tradition"—that existed before there were concentrated bodies of civil society where human beings became highly organized in large numbers. Even anciently, people were

---

*Notes to the text of *The Ancient Walk-About Way* appear on pp. 110–12.

being religious. In fact, ancient peoples were being everything that human beings, generally speaking, are now. Even the ancient, prehistoric peoples are part of the Great Tradition. The Great Tradition of humankind is a universal tradition, because it is based on the One Reality—not only the Great, Indivisible Non-conditional Reality, but also the unity of conditional existence and the commonality and unity of human beings themselves.

—Avatar Adi Da Samraj
September 8, 2004

The Bringer of Light in the Darkness

In the first of this collection of writings, Adi Da describes His function as the Sunlight that opens the eyes of those who are asleep. In fact, the Sanskrit word "Guru" literally indicates the dispelling of darkness.

> *The syllable gu means shadows,*
> *The syllable ru, he who disperses them.*
> *Because of the power to disperse darkness*
> *the guru is thus named.*[3]

The function of Guru has appeared in almost every esoteric (or really Truth-Realizing) form of human Spiritual practice. From Buddhist masters and Hindu Siddhas to the Jewish Zaddiks, Christian Spiritual fathers, and Muslim shaykhs, the transformative relationship to the illumined guide is testimony to the universal truth of the "ancient Walk-About Way".

Avatar Adi Da once described the "physics" of the Guru-devotee relationship as a "law of vibration". When one object vibrating at a particular frequency is brought into proximity with another such object, the second object can begin to vibrate "in tune" with the first. The Guru appears in

human form, but not in the ordinary human state. The Guru
is one who is—to one or another great degree—beyond limitation, and thus literally "vibrates" a State of Realization. The
devotee comes into the Company of the Guru, and what is
communicated is not an exchange with a separate, "other"
human being, but rather the Guru's Realization itself. By
spending time with the Guru, the devotee who does not
"hold on" to self (and thus stop the process of "sympathetic
vibration") becomes more and more resonant with the Guru's
State. The human Guru is thus a profound help to human
beings, because the Guru appears in human form to communicate that which is otherwise beyond human experience.

The spontaneous recognition of the Guru as the
Revealer of Truth is the basis on which the ancient Walk-
About Way was embraced. And to truly live the relationship
with the Guru to fullest advantage, human beings must
embrace a mature and self-responsible habit of living.

The "Radical" Revelation of Reality Itself

Although there is a Great Tradition of response to Truth,
even in relationship to the human Guru, it is also obvious
that human beings have a penchant for creating and living
in bondage and suffering. Thus, Adi Da Samraj has Given a
full Teaching that addresses every aspect of human experience. Relative to all religious and Spiritual traditions, He
describes a three-part paradigm of (1) presumed separate
(and subjective) self, (2) presumed separate (and objective)
world, and (3) presumed separate "God" or Great State. Of
course, the presumption of an irreconcilable difference
between what is subjective and objective is so obvious a
feature of our experience that we tend not to question it at
all. But the presumed split between self and world and
"God" is the essential problem that human philosophy and
religious endeavor seek to resolve.

Avatar Adi Da has made a supremely "radical" Revelation about the nature of the self we presume to be, and which we presume is inherently "different" from everything else. The separate self (or ego-"I") is, He says, not something we are <u>being</u>. Rather, the separate "self" (or ego-"I") is something we are <u>doing</u>. Or, as Adi Da has said countless times, "The ego is not an <u>entity</u>, but an <u>activity</u>."

The root-activity of the ego is what Adi Da describes as self-contraction. Presuming to be a separate (and, therefore, inherently threatened) "someone", every human being contracts (physically, emotionally, mentally, and with the breath) in the face of the apparent threat of everything "other". However, that activity of self-contraction is <u>not</u> inherent to the being. That activity of self-contraction is something each human being is doing in reaction to his or her (real or presumed) experience.

The Way of Adidam, which Avatar Adi Da has Revealed and Given, is the Way of the "radical" (or "at-the-root") transcending of the self-contraction. Only when such "radical" ego-transcendence is the case is it possible to truly "Know" Reality Itself. Thus, the "radical" transcending of egoity is an absolutely essential aspect of the Ultimate Reality-Realizing process of Adidam Offered to all by Adi Da Samraj.

Devotion, Right Life, and "Perfect Knowledge" in the Walk-About Way of Adidam

In the later essays of *The Ancient Walk-About Way*, Adi Da elucidates the fundamental elements of the Way of Adidam He has Given: devotion, right life, and "Perfect Knowledge".

The tacit, non-verbal heart-response of devotion to Adi Da Samraj is (from the beginning and always) the basis of Adidam. To live that Way in its fullness is to extend devotional recognition of Adi Da Samraj into an active response of every aspect of the being—"inner" and "outer"—via a comprehensive discipline of right life. The life of Adi Da's devotee is converted from the habit-patterns based in identification with the separative body-mind to the disposition of all action as service to the Divine Heart-Master and His Liberating Work.

The enactment of right life serves to magnify the intuition of Truth that is inherent in devotion to Adi Da Samraj. Thus, His Revelation of "Perfect Knowledge" is ever-magnified—at first via a preparatory practice and, ultimately (by His Grace) as Perfect Identification with His "Bright" Divine State.

The disposition of right practice of The Way of Adidam simply "Coincides" with Me—In "Place" ("Where" and As I Am).

—Avatar Adi Da Samraj
"In 'Place' ('Where' and As I Am)"

The Seventh Stage Way

Adi Da's schema of seven stages of life (see pp. 118–21) is another crucial element of His Communication in this book. As He Reveals, the Great Tradition of human religious and Spiritual endeavor—historical and prehistorical—is founded on the structures and processes inherent in the human being.

The seven stages of life I have Described develop on the basis of the structures of the true (or esoteric) "anatomy" of every human being. Every human activity and every human manifestation can be seen and understood in the context of My Description of the seven stages of life and the associated structural "anatomy" of the human being.

—Avatar Adi Da Samraj
September 8, 2004

In His description of the first six stages of life, Adi Da illuminates how the pursuits of religion and Spirituality (both

Eastern and Western) have always been focused in different dimensions of the human structure—whether associated with the gross or the subtle or the causal dimension of existence.[4] By contrast, the Way of Adidam is the "seventh stage Way"—a process that is, from the beginning and always, not based on any gross, subtle, or causal structure of the body-mind, but on direct and free heart-response to the Perfect Divine Reality Itself, Revealed in and as the Bodily Form of Adi Da Samraj.

One who most fully responds to Adi Da Samraj knows that nothing can be done to and as the separate body-mind-self in order to Realize the Truth of His Divine State. Any strategic manipulation of the body-mind merely reinforces the ego. Therefore, in the Walk-About Way of devotion to Adi Da, the devotee simply ceases to give attention to the patterns and sufferings of identification with body, mind, "self", and world, and instead turns the total body-mind to Adi Da. Through this conversion from self-obsession to true devotion, the devotee is purified by means of Avatar Adi Da's Divine Grace. Such devotion necessarily occurs prior to any form of identification with body, mind, or "self". It is in this sense that devotion to Adi Da Samraj is "radical"—because that devotion happens in the root-"Place" of Reality Itself.

Those who heart-recognize Me . . . are recognizing (or tacitly Apprehending) My Divine State. Such heart-recognition is "radical" devotion—because such heart-recognition of Me is already "at the root". In that case, there is no body-mind-ego responding to Me. Rather, there is direct heart-recognition of Me—Prior to all identification with the body-mind, and Prior to all identification with the patterning of the body-mind.

—Avatar Adi Da Samraj
"In 'Place' ('Where' and As I Am)"

The Divine Avataric Intervention

Only One Present as Reality Itself—That Which Simply Is, Prior to mind and any "point of view"—can Reveal the Perfect Truth. Human beings cannot punch their way out of the bag of their fixed and separate viewpoints. They must be Shown Reality and Helped to Realize It. That is the import of the Divine and Avataric Revelation of Adi Da Samraj.

There is no way to adequately capture in words the richness and joy of the relationship with Adi Da Samraj. And yet that great relationship is evident in every sign of life as His devotee. His Teaching is a Work of genius that breaks down the barriers of language to communicate the Indescribable. He is not separate from anyone or anything—and He demonstrates this to His devotee through constant synchronicities of His Regard. He grows and purifies every talent and offering His devotee lays before Him in service. He Grants heart-breaking Blessing of those who are suffering in body, emotion, or mind. His Sublime Company Radiates the Love-Bliss-Stillness of His Divine State of Being.

Heart-liberation is instant from the sight of Adi Da Samraj, and the ultimate and permanent Freedom He Offers is manifested by His Grace over time. In response to the certainty of the Divine through heart-recognition of Adi Da Samraj as the Divine Avataric Intervention, life thus becomes simply a theatre in which to constantly cultivate and create opportunity for magnifying the relationship with Him. Most importantly, Adi Da Samraj is here to make possible the Gift of Most Perfect Realization of the Divine Reality for those who embrace Him most seriously. His Gift of "Open Eyes" Reveals all experience as utterly transparent to the Divine Reality That Is Always Already the Case. ∎

I Am The One
Who Would Awaken You

1.

The usual person thinks: "This body and its psyche are dying. This world is dying. Everyone is suffering. Everyone is seeking. There is mortality. There is frustration and limitation." But none of that is Truth. Those interpretations are not Truth. The world itself is not Truth—nor is life, nor psyche and body, nor death, nor experience. No event is, in and of itself, Truth. Everything that arises is an appearance to Consciousness Itself, a modification of the Divine Conscious Light That Is Always Already the Case.

All of this is a dream, if you like. It is an appearance in Consciousness Itself. Truth Is Very Consciousness Itself. Truth is to all of this what the waking state is to the dreaming state. If you awaken, you do not have to do anything about the condition you may have suffered or enjoyed in the dream state. What happened within the dream is suddenly not your present condition. It is of no consequence any longer, once you are awake.

If you persist in dreaming, and your "point of view" remains that of the dreamer (and the dreamer's role within the dream), then your possible actions are numberless. But none of them will "work". They will simply occupy you in the dream. They will modify the dream state, but no action in the dream is the equivalent of waking. There are simply forms of fascination, of occupation, of seeking—until you wake up.

Truth is simply Waking, No-illusion. It is not a condition within this appearance. It has nothing whatsoever to do with the mind, regardless of whether the mind is expanded or contracted.

There is One Who is Wide Awake while He Appears in the dream. By not supporting the dream, He Awakens others. He Is the True Divine Guru. I _Am_ That One.

The significance of My Work is not in anything I do _within_ the dream. I simply do not support it. I do not live as it. I do not believe it. I do not take it seriously. Apparently, I can feel and act as I please within the dream. I persist in the common (or ordinary) manner. But I do not support the dream. I do not live from its "point of view". I do not live its structure to others. I do not live the self-contraction to others—the avoidance of relationship, the separate-self-sense.

Simply because I live in this manner, those who are devotionally related to Me tend to become Awake. But, while they are Awakening, they persist in dreaming to various degrees. Forms of the dream persist. The search persists. Often, they get a little distance from the dream—it seems to break up at times, seems to disappear. It becomes vague, it becomes uninteresting, it becomes unserious, it becomes serious again.

You are just beginning to Awaken. Heart-Communion with Me is the dream in which I Appear. Now it is as if you are beginning to wake up in your room. You are in bed, and it is morning. There are a few things you begin to notice, which indicate that you are in another state. Those who are Awakening in Truth begin to notice something. They begin to recognize the signs. They begin to recognize the activity of dreaming. They begin to sense something very unusual about Me.

Before their actual Awakening, I appear as all kinds of things to them. I suggest all kinds of fantastic things. All the things they can imagine while they dream, everything unbelievable, is what they think I am. I may appear to be extraordinary, a doer of famous things. I may appear playfully as that. But I Am simply Awake. Not a single thing is happening. Not a single thing has been accomplished. I Am Only Awake.

I am like the sunlight in the morning. I Intensify the light of morning until you Awaken. Until the Light Awakens you, even the Light of Consciousness Itself, you continue to dream, try to survive within the dream, manipulate yourself within the dream, pursue all kinds of goals, searches—none of which Awaken you.

The ordinary means only console you and distract you within the dream. I Myself, the One Who would Awaken you, am not a person, not an individual within the dream. I Am your Very Consciousness. I Am Reality Itself, the Divine Conscious Light, the True Waking State, the True Divine Heart—Breaking Through the force of dreaming. It is not that you are some poor person who needs some other poor person to help you out. It may appear to be so within the dream—but, in Reality, I Am your own True Self-Nature Appearing within the dream to Awaken you. I Am your Awakening, and your Always Already Conscious State.

Even while dreaming, you may experience suggestions of waking. You may become momentarily aware of the body, momentarily aware of lying in bed. For a moment, the images of the dream may stop. Likewise, I Myself, Appearing within the world, Am truly your Real Conscious State. My Person in the world is like an image in a dream. But, in fact, I am more like your moments of wakening awareness—the moments that move you into the waking state. I am not some separateness, some individual. I Am Consciousness Itself, Reality Itself, Truth Itself.

2.

In heart-Communion with Me, the Truth is Lived to you—and you then live the Truth as your Condition. Gradually, you become less and less involved with the suffering-and-seeking images of yourself. You become less concerned with the usual process of your life. You are doing less and less about it. You are trying less and less to get free, to get Realized, to get to God, Liberation, and pleasant sensation. You are not trying to stop engaging all of that effort. It just begins to wear down, while you live the conditions

Given by Me. You simply notice this. You cease to be occupied with your search—because the Truth is being Lived to you. The Truth is being Lived <u>as</u> yourself, by Means of My Divine Avataric Grace.

That Realization Which does not support separation and seeking is the ground of "radical" self-understanding. In heart-Communion with Me, that Realization replaces the ordinary operating basis of your life. You simply forget your adventure of suffering—that is all. The Power of heart-Communion with Me distracts you from mere suffering (or the separate and separative and always seeking body-mind-self)—until Truth Itself becomes Obvious.

Therefore, Truth is not a matter of doing something <u>to</u> the ego, the separate-self-sense, the identification with the body, or anything else. Rather, Truth is simply to be lived—because Truth obviates all that is not Truth.

I Live the Divine Force, and Generate the conditions, of Spiritual life in relationship to My devotee. Over time, more and more responsibility is given to My devotee—in the course of deepening devotion to Me and increasing self-discipline, self-understanding, and self-transcendence (or Real ego-transcendence). The process of the heart-relationship with Me is a Divine Gift, Avatarically Given by Me—a Gift That is progressively more and more profound.

3.

I have talked about the relationship between Guru and devotee as the essence, the fundamental condition, of Spiritual practice. But the Guru-devotee relationship is not a form of concentration on the Guru as a separate (and merely symbolic) entity. That is not relationship. That is your own fabrication, your own suffering again. Whenever there is relationship, there is no need for all of these symbolic constructs. The true nature of Spiritual practice in My Divine

Avataric Heart-Company is to live the <u>Condition</u> (and the <u>life-conditions</u>) of heart-Communion with Me, of relationship to Me in My Function as True Divine Guru.

Within the dream, the potential images may be consoling, and even hopeful—but such consolation or hope is not the equivalent of being Awake. Consolation and hope <u>depend</u> upon your being asleep. The forms of seeking exploit your capability to identify with the fundamental dilemma of dreaming, which is its unconsciousness. The forms of seeking may satisfy you within the context of your presumptions, but they are not the equivalent of Waking Up.

What is required to Wake Up? What can you do within the dream to Wake Up? Not a thing. There is only the Waking Itself. All actions within the dream are forms of the dream itself. Waking is another process—and It occurs by other means, by Divinely Graceful Means.

I am not a symbol, a condition of the dream itself. No mere symbol, no mere condition of the dream, can Wake you Up. I <u>Am</u> the Divine Conscious Light, the Real Divine Person—Always Already Awake, Functioning Alive. I Appear in bodily (human) Form, within the dream of life—not in order to console you, but to Awaken you through the Real crisis in consciousness. I am a frustration to the unconscious condition of the dream.

I <u>Am</u> the Man of "Radical" Understanding. In My Function as the True Divine Guru, I <u>Am</u> the Divine Awakener. I <u>Am</u> the Person of Reality Itself.

I Am Always Already Awake. I could not care less about your urges and demands within the dream. I refuse to satisfy them. I refuse to give you an experience merely to console you. I have no intention of satisfying anyone's egoic game. All the demands for satisfaction that you bring are frustrated in My Company. What is satisfied, what is made to grow, is that fundamental Intuition of Reality that is already the Foundation of your existence. That Intuition is intensified in heart-Communion with Me. All the rest, the fascinated search, begins to fall away. In heart-Communion with Me, the search begins to reveal itself, until it becomes obvious.

4.

Only the seeker takes the dilemma seriously. The waking state does not take your dreams seriously. It is not the least concerned with your dreams. And, fortunately, all beings are already alive with the Intuition of Reality. Therefore, all beings have an affinity with Sunlight, with the True Waking State—with Me. Unqualified Reality, the Love-Bliss-Happiness of My "Bright" Divine Self-Condition, is What they are already living—and that is What is consciously discovered in the heart-relationship to Me. Because you Always Already Inhere in My Love-Bliss-Happiness, I Draw you to <u>Myself</u>.

It is the Intuition of Reality Itself that inexorably draws people to Me, that leads them to maintain themselves in My Divine Avataric Heart-Company. All apparent "reasons" for holding on to Me fall away, and also all the apparent "reasons" for not holding on to Me. None of these reasons has any ultimate significance. It is your inherent affinity for Truth, your Intuition of the Divine Self-Condition, of the Living Divine Heart Itself, that is entirely responsible for the practice in My Divine Avataric Heart-Company.

When you become less concerned with your particular search, your inwardness, your adventure, then you have simply become more sensitive to your Real Condition. You have felt the sunlight falling on your sleeping eyes. When your eyes have opened in the morning light, everything will be obvious to you—and you will know that you have never slept, that you have never dreamed, that you have never been limited to any thing that has appeared. You have never been limited to any condition that you have presumed. There was always only Reality Itself, the True Divine Self-Nature of all-and-All—Which Is Love-Bliss-Happiness Itself, Consciousness Itself, the Unqualified Presence of Reality Itself, Truth Itself, and Real (Acausal) God.

I <u>Am</u> That.

The Super-Physics
of Divine Enlightenment

Divine Self-Realization is absolutely uncommon. In Its Most Perfect Completeness, It has, until My Own Divine Avataric Appearance and Demonstration, never transpired in anyone's case in the entire history of the human world.[5] It is, rather, a process that belongs to the future "evolution" of humanity—at best, thousands, millions, billions of years in the future, for the human race as a whole.

At present, almost all human beings persist in an infantile developmental moment that has nothing whatsoever to do with the Ultimate Truth. As a general rule, human beings are still dependent, violent, ego-possessed—still seeking consolations in the realm of changes. Therefore, do not imagine for a moment that the only-by-Me Revealed and Given Way of Adidam is an easy matter, that you can simply listen to My Teaching-Argument and (thereby) Realize the Divine Self-Condition. The Way of Adidam is the Work of Reality Itself. The Way of Adidam is the obligation (or Law) of Eternal Existence—an obligation generated, and regenerated, by the heart-relationship to Me.

The humanly incarnate Spiritual Master is Divine Help to the advantage of those in like form. When My devotee enters into right relationship with Me, changes happen in the literal physics of one's existence. I am not just talking about ideas. I am Talking about literal transformations at the level of energy, at the level of esoteric super-physics (beyond the physical limitations you characteristically presume), at the level of the Unqualified Condition of the Divine Conscious Light. That transformative process is enacted in My devotees in (and by Means of) My Divine Avataric Company.

The relationship between the Adept-Realizer and the devotee is not a matter of conceptual symbolisms or emotional attachment to some extraordinary person. The true Guru-devotee relationship is real physics. Therefore, because human beings can make unique use of the Offering of the Adept-Realizer's Company, it is to the special advantage of people when a Realizer-Guru (of whatever Real degree) appears in their midst. And that advantage is Unique in My Case, because I have Revealed and Given the <u>Complete</u> Process, Which culminates in Most Perfect (or seventh stage) Divine Self-Realization.

Spiritual life has nothing to do with the childishness people tend to dramatize in relationship to the Spiritual Master. I Criticize that childish (or dependent) approach more directly than most people do. Others are merely petulant about the necessity of the relationship to the Spiritual Master, in the self-righteous mood of adolescence. Both the childish approach and the adolescent approach to the Spiritual Master are forms of destructive nonsense and must be overcome.[6] However, the mature, ego-surrendering relationship to the Spiritual Master is absolutely Lawful and necessary. Those who object to that relationship might as well object to the relationship between the Earth and the Sun.

Most people are willing to sacrifice <u>things</u>, but not themselves. They are willing to pay cash, in other words, for a quick salvation. Such "religious consumerism" is an ancient ritual of worship, but it is false and futile. True worship is the surrender of your own body-mind in Truth, in the Living and Transformative Company of the Spiritual Master. People absolutely resist such surrender, because they know nothing about it. Human beings are, in fact, subhuman in their present level of adaptation. Devotional surrender of the egoic self represents a future stage of development for humanity as a species. In their present actual, literal, psycho-physical condition, human beings are incapable of such surrender. They must be drawn out of that limited condition, and into another state of existence. And it is as far to go from where they are now to Most Ultimate Divine Self-Realization as it is from the amoeba in the primal mud of the Earth to a human being. Every aspect of your existence—even the body— must change dramatically.

There is an unspeakably profound difference between the condition of the usual egoic individual and the Condition of the Divinely Enlightened individual. If imagined in "evolutionary" terms, that difference is an inconceivable leap. However, there is a real process for making that leap, and there is Help for it: the devotional and (in due course) Spiritual relationship to Me, the Divine Siddha-Guru. In other words, something in the Super-Physics of the universe makes it possible for the Divine Conscious Light to Avatarically Incarnate as an apparent human individual, for the Purpose of Bringing others into the Sphere of Divinely Enlightened Existence. Therefore, just as the relationship to the Spiritual Master (of one or another degree) is the Supreme Principle of Spiritual life in general, the relationship to Me is the Supreme Principle of the Way of Adidam.

True Spiritual life is not just a change in your mind. Much more than an "inner awakening" or a "good feeling" about everything must take place. The literal physics of your entire existence must change. The physical body and its energies must be literally transformed. Spiritual processes do not occur as a result of the "subjective" nonsense of vicarious belief and vicarious salvation that people usually associate with religion—as if Real Awakening were merely a matter of asking some silly question or going to a few lectures for the weekend.

That is not Divine Enlightenment. Divine Enlightenment is a literal change of the <u>whole</u> <u>body</u>. If you have acquired the human form, then the change that must occur in the body is not really so much in your outward appearance, because you already have the necessary structure. Rather, the changes that must occur are psycho-physical changes— just as literal as if you were to acquire more legs and arms, except that the most dramatic changes occur in dimensions other than the shape of the physical body. Changes certainly do occur in the flesh and in the elemental structures of the body, but those changes do not really alter the body's outward shape. Nevertheless, those changes are as literal as the "evolutionary" change from a dinosaur to a human being—and they are as dramatic as that, but they principally occur at more subtle levels of the physics of the conditional being. There are literal changes in the nervous system, literal changes in the chemistry of the body, literal changes in the structural functioning of the brain.[7]

You cannot realize such changes in a weekend. They are a living process of growth—but they can be quickened and intensified through right practice, and real ego-transcending discipline, in My Divine Avataric Company. I Communicate My Own "Bright" Divine Self-Condition to you, thereby Effecting a "radical" (or "at-the-root") transformation in the disposition of your body-mind. And, then (over time), I Magnify the effectiveness of that disposition many times, such that the entire Process of Divine Enlightenment may take place even in a single lifetime—or (at least) be dramatically advanced in one lifetime, if not completely fulfilled.

In the Literature of My Divine Avataric Wisdom-Teaching, I have Described the full esoteric progression of this remarkable transformation.[8] My Description is not based on any mere intellectual synthesis of things I have read and thought about. The entire process of the Way of Adidam is My literal Experience. My Divine Avataric Wisdom-Teaching brings the significance of all the patterns of existence into a clear unity, such that the entire affair of human existence can be approached rightly. Constant Self-Abiding <u>As</u> the "Bright" (Itself) Is My Very Existence. And the Power of My Spiritual Transmission of the "Bright" is available for the transformation of others—if people will enter into devotional (and, in due course, Spiritual) relationship with Me.

If you enter into the heart-relationship with Me, then the Divine Process begins to duplicate Itself in your case. It is not as if you are a robot that is being transformed through the effect of some computer—no. The Process is a living and human relationship with Me. But that Process has nothing to do with the conventional "doctor-patient" and "mommy-daddy-baby" games. Irresponsible people cannot enter into this Process. You must be responsible for yourself at the human level, and in a profoundly uncommon way. You must live the discipline of ordinary life. You yourself must <u>be</u> love under all ordinary, daily conditions. You must make this change in your life. There is no way whereby you can be relieved of this necessity—and nobody else can do it for you. Nevertheless, all of that ordinary responsibility simply prepares you for the right relationship to Me (in and <u>As</u> My Avatarically-Born bodily human Divine Form and Person).

I Am your Unique Advantage, because I Am Present in the same kind of bodily form as you—Manifested in the same kind of physical condition, the same kind of nervous system, the same kind of brain. In My Case, however, all these mechanisms are Raised to an Absolute level of Functioning, such that your entering into Communion with Me brings changes even at the level of the psycho-physical body that you present to Me.

No abstract Divine Principle can serve you in that manner, because the physics of this Process must be directly Present, and the bodily (human) Demonstration of the Process must be Present in a Form that can Do Its Work in your case. That Work is My Purpose. My Divine Avataric Incarnation Fully Manifests the State of the Ultimate Physics of things—Which is your Potential, but not your actuality at the present time. The "abstract Divine" and the powers of the universe are not (in and of themselves) organized for the sake of the immediate transformation of human beings. If people truly enter into right devotional and (in due course) Spiritual relationship with Me, they will (inevitably) Realize the progressive process of transformation characteristic of the only-by-Me Revealed and Given Way of Adidam.

I Am here to Reveal the Perfect Teaching of Truth and to Initiate the great culture of compassion and Wisdom among human beings. However, those Purposes are secondary aspects of My Divine Avataric Service to humanity. Those Purposes are the Transformative Effects of My "Bright" Divine State and My Ultimate Divine Function. My True and Ultimate Divine Avataric Function is to Instigate the Super-Physics of Most Perfect Real-God-Realization (or Divine Enlightenment) among My true devotees.

My Avataric Self-Manifestation in bodily (human) Divine Form is an Advantage That is Unique in human time.

I Am
Your Unique
Advantage

Real (Acausal) God is not at the end of the Way of Adidam. Real (Acausal) God is at the very beginning of the Way of Adidam. I Come to you directly. I Descend and Enter into your life. I am not merely calling to you from Beyond, or giving you a philosophy. I have Entered fully into the cosmic domain. I Am Fully <u>here</u>. All you need do, in any moment, is Find Me in My Divine Attractiveness. Find Me by Communing with Me. You need not be concerned with how much concentration of mind there is, how much poetic vision there is, how much relaxation there is in the body, how pleasant the conditions of life are. You need not be concerned with the fact that life is difficult at the moment, or that you yourself are obnoxious. You need not be concerned about any of it! All of that content is simply the inevitable suffering that is the result of conditional existence. All you need do is Find <u>Me</u>—by Means of heart-Communion with Me. Be Attracted to <u>Me</u>, and let the body-mind be changed by My Divine Avataric Spiritual Self-Transmission. Such is the Principle of the devotional (and, in due course, Spiritual) relationship to Me. Such is the Principle of the only-by-Me Revealed and Given Way of Adidam. Because of That Principle, I Am your Unique (Divine Avataric) Advantage.

There is one Great Law: You become what you meditate on.

This Law summarizes the Process whereby I can Be your Unique Advantage. In the midst of perceiving beings and things and phenomena of all kinds, My true devotee is always in heart-Communion with Me. As My true devotee, you are always concentrated in Me. In the midst of whatever arises, you constantly turn whole bodily to Me.

When you Behold Me with devotion, you are Beholding the Divine Reality Itself—in Its Fullness and Perfection. When you Behold Me, you are Beholding the All-Completing Divine Avataric Self-Revelation.

Therefore, I Am your Unique (Divine Avataric) Advantage. Simply by Means of your heart-Communion with Me (in all the moments of conditional existence), the total Process in My Divine Avataric Company is progressively Activated in you, by My Divine Avataric Spiritual Grace. The developmental stages of practice in the only-by-Me Revealed and Given Way of Adidam[9] will be spontaneously manifested in you—not by your self-consciously duplicating the signs of each of those stages, but merely by your consistently entering into heart-Communion with Me.

To the degree that you are reluctant to Behold Me with full feeling-devotion, to the degree that you stand aloof in your egoic self, your participation in Me is limited. In that case, you merely struggle with the egoic stages of life, very much involved in your egoic self.

I Am your Unique (Divine Avataric) Advantage—but not because I Give you a process that you can successfully apply to yourself, if only you will bear down and muster enough effort. I specifically do <u>not</u> offer any such ego-driven process. I Am your Unique Advantage because I Offer you a <u>relationship</u> to Me. Heart-Communion with Me makes the process of the Way of Adidam unique—and capable of being fulfilled instantly, directly. In actual practice, some time is (of course) involved—because of the limitations in your devotion to Me. However, when I Speak of your practice of the Way of Adidam, I am not speaking of your continued conditional reappearances ad infinitum (in numberless lifetimes). I am Speaking of a process that may (at least potentially) be fulfilled even in your present lifetime. If you will truly use your Unique Advantage (with full understanding of what your relationship to Me is all about), the significance of this relationship will be fully Revealed to you.

In that case, you will truly understand that to practice the Way of Adidam is simply to Behold Me with full heart-feeling, to turn to Me whole bodily (with mind, emotion, physical body, and breath). Then the various dimensions of My Divine Avataric Sign will spontaneously become apparent to you, and your devotional life will be full—not by your own effort, but entirely by My Divine Avataric Grace.

Heart-Communion with Me is the one necessary qualification for practice of the Way of Adidam. You must be invested in Me as your Unique Advantage. The direct Way in My Divine Avataric Company is most intimate heart-Communion with Me. Indeed, it has been known since the ancient days that the Way of heart-Communion with the Adept Spiritual Master is the <u>only</u> true esoteric Process of Real-God-Realization. In this aggressively exoteric "late-time" (or "dark" epoch), I have restored that great and ancient Process—and, by virtue of My Perfect Self-Abidance in My Own "Bright" Divine Self-Condition, My Offering of the great esoteric Process of heart-Communion with Me is the Perfect Fulfillment of all true esotericism. Therefore, from this time forward, all beings have the opportunity to directly enter into the true Spiritual (and, Ultimately, Most Perfectly Real-God-Realizing) Process—simply by means of true heart-Communion with Me (as My true—and, necessarily, formally practicing—devotees).

What must change through heart-Communion with Me is your fundamental sense of the Divine Reality. If you are established in That in any moment (regardless of what is happening in the body-mind), you will (thereby) Realize the Love-Bliss-Happiness, the Inherent Freedom, of Self-Existing and Self-Radiant Divine Being Itself. You will also inevitably show, in your present lifetime, the signs of effective movement through the developmental stages of practice—I Guarantee it! There are no two ways about it. The Process of the Divine Enlightenment of the body-mind is a more predictable Process than any science on Earth. The Way of Adidam is an exact and Perfectly Effective Science—if it can be called a "science" at all, since it is not based on the obsession with maintaining an "objective" stance. Whoever you are, there is no possibility that that Great Divine Process will not work in your case. <u>No</u> possibility. <u>No</u> <u>one</u> is damned. <u>No</u> <u>one</u> is inherently (or essentially) limited.

Each person, by virtue of his or her appearance, shows whatever Spiritual signs he or she presently shows. Thus, in any particular moment, some appear to be in a better position than others. Nevertheless, in relation to Me, there are no limits. All are Given My Divine Avataric Grace fully, openly, without limitation. Your potential Realization is not, in any sense, limited by your karmic (or conditional) state.

Basically, you must be responsible for turning the principal faculties to Me—and, Ultimately, you must utterly transcend them (including even attention itself), in Most Perfect Self-Identification with Me. My Divine Avataric Grace Is here. My Divine Avataric Grace is Given. I Am here for everyone—exactly, Personally, and directly. But if you are irresponsible in relationship to Me, if you insist on remaining ego-possessed, you cannot receive My Divine Avataric Grace. In that case, you do not allow Me to Do My Divine Avataric Work in your own body-mind.

My Divine Avataric Work takes place in your own body-mind, presently. My Divine Avataric Work is not merely something that occurred once and must now be commemorated for thousands of years. My Divine Avataric Work is continuous, forever.

Turn to <u>Me</u>, in heart-Communion with <u>Me</u>. Let heart-Communion with Me be your discipline in every moment—most profoundly, fully, constantly, without any effort at all. There is no effort associated with turning the principal faculties to Me. Nothing is easier than turning the body-mind to That Which Is Supremely Attractive.

Behold Me with feeling-devotion. I <u>Am</u> your Real Divine Self-Condition. Therefore, you must always turn to Me, and then allow your psycho-physical patterning time to change.

Do not make practice into the observation of changes in the body-mind. Let practice be the constant event of Beholding the One Who Is Attractive. <u>That</u> is practice in My Divine Avataric Company.

The Supreme Secret
of Spiritual Life

What is Supremely Attractive in the conditional universe and in the human world is the God-Man. All beings, male and female, must become Distracted by That One. Divine Distraction is the Supreme Yoga. For this reason, the Divine Appears in conditional Form, in the likeness of those who are to be Drawn out of bondage—but only in their likeness. It is the <u>Divine</u> That Appears in that likeness, and it is the <u>Divine</u> That is made Visible through that likeness.

Those who become capable of heart-recognizing Me As That Supremely Attractive One also (thereby) become capable of heart-responding to Me (the Divine Avataric Self-Revelation of the Divine Being, Truth, and Reality)—and, by becoming My formal devotees, they become participants in the Walk-About Way of Adidam, Which I Offer to all beings. The Way of Adidam truly is the Way of Divine Grace, because It requires no effort at all. It requires nothing but My Divine Avataric Grace and the heart-response to My Divine Avataric Grace. Responding to Grace is not effortful—except for those who refuse to do it. To respond to Grace is easy—because it is easy to respond to That Which is Supremely Attractive.

The only-by-Me Revealed and Given Way of Adidam is as I have always Described it. The only-by-Me Revealed and Given Way of Adidam is the devotional and, in due course, Spiritual relationship to Me, the Divine Heart-Master. That relationship takes the form of a life of practice, a life of disciplines (including the discipline of meditation, or, as the case may be, "Perfect Contemplation"[10])—all of which disciplines are true and useful, and all of which disciplines are necessary to Real religious and Spiritual life. But the Essence of all such disciplines is Divine Distraction.

Those who are Distracted by Me are Distracted by My Avatarically-Born bodily (human) Divine Form, My Avatarically Self-Transmitted Divine Spiritual Presence, and My Avatarically Self-Revealed Divine and Perfect State.

Through the Real Process of devotional recognition-response to Me, they enter into heart-Communion with Me, the Avatarically Incarnate Divine Person. Worldly people want nothing to do with that Process—and, likewise, worldly religionists, scholars, pundits, and ego-possessed "guru"-figures want nothing to do with It. Nevertheless, the Supreme Secret of religious and Spiritual life is Distraction by the God-Man.

However, even though this Secret has been Communicated in many times and places, It has been understood and truly Realized by very few. Both men and women must be Distracted by the God-Man (or the Avataric Incarnation of the Divine Person). They must turn to That Which is Supremely Attractive, and they must love That One. By virtue of their surrender to the Divine Avataric Incarnation, people can truly love one another and others and this world. If they cannot or will not be Distracted by the God-Man, then they cannot get out of the purgatory that is this conditional realm. At best, they will practice the disciplines that are associated with the Way of Truth in a willful (or egoic) manner. At worst, they will simply become dissociated, and convince themselves that there is no Great Distraction, no Real (Acausal) God, no Truth, and then commit themselves to self-indulgence and to the conventional destiny.

When you try to break through the ego's dilemmas yourself, to discover the Truth yourself, you find that you cannot do any such thing—not to the degree of Most Perfect Divine Self-Realization. That discovery breaks the heart and makes it possible for you to be Distracted by What Is Beyond your egoic self, and to make right and true use of your relationship to Me, such that your relationship to Me becomes ecstatic.

My Function as the Divine Heart-Master is to Manifest My Divine Avataric Self-Revelation in present-time, in relationship to living beings. As the Divine Heart-Master, I Am Indefinable—not a "thing", not a defined "subject", not a ritual and cultic "object". I Am Utterly Incomprehensible, beyond any possible definition. Thus, when you enter ecstatically into the heart-relationship to Me, you move completely beyond whatever limitations you (as ego-"I") may tend to assume about Me (as an apparent human being). My Avatarically-Born bodily (human) Divine Form Is the by-Me-Avatarically-Self-Manifested Divine Means for your Distraction in Me—and the entire devotional and Spiritual Process in My Divine Avataric Company is just such Distraction.

Real Spiritual life is founded in Love-Communion with the Divine, and absolute dependence on Divine Grace. Love-Communion with Me is dependence on My Divine Avataric Grace. Love-Communion with Me is the Beholding of My Avatarically Self-Revealed Divinity in living terms—not just in "subjective", mystical terms (as if you were sitting somewhere, removed from life), but in all the circumstances of your life. The Way of Divine Communion is the Way of the devotional and Spiritual relationship to Me (in and As My Avatarically-Born bodily human Divine Form and Person), not an endless excursion of wandering in your psyche.

To be My devotee is to surrender to Me, to live your dependence on Me, your love of Me, your Distraction by Me. If you are My devotee, Love-Communion with Me (in and As My Avatarically-Born Bodily Human Divine Form and Person) must always be established now and moment to moment. Only in that case can your practice in My Divine Avataric Company be true.

The entire purpose of everything that occurs between Me and My devotee is the establishment of this "in-Love" relationship. Without that relationship, there is no Spiritual practice. All My devotees must enjoy such Distraction, whether or not they ever come into My Divine Avataric physical human Company. All the conditions of your life and every moment of your life must be a form of service to Me, a form of heart-Communion with Me, a form of connection with

Me—in and <u>As</u> My Avatarically-Born bodily (human) Divine Form and Person.

My true devotee becomes more and more Enchanted by My Divine Avataric Company. Whose Company are you in? You are in <u>My</u> Company. I am Personally in your company As That Which is Boundlessly Attractive. I <u>Am</u> all beings, all body-minds. I am not merely speaking a metaphor. What I am Describing is literally the Case—absolutely, literally, the Case. That Force of Being Which is Manifested as everything is That Which is Absolutely Attractive.

All My devotees are Drawn to Me by Means of My Divine Attractiveness. They become transformed by just That. In the only-by-Me Revealed and Given Way of Adidam, the <u>Essence</u> of your practice is your Attractedness to Me.

That "Intoxicating"[11] Attractiveness, That completely Overwhelming Whirl of My Spirit-Force, My Love-Bliss, My Happiness—by Means of Which I (Most Ultimately) Draw you into My "Bright" Divine Spherical Self-Domain—Is the Essence of the only-by-Me Revealed and Given Way of Adidam. I have Described the Process in My Divine Avataric Company in full technical detail—but the Essence of the Way of Adidam is Attraction to Me, an Overwhelming Attraction to Me, an Attraction that eventually begins to ruin the ego-life you are otherwise perpetuating. Your Attraction to Me becomes an Influence that Shatters all the conventional arrangements and strategies by which you (as ego-"I") try to "feel good".

That Supremely Attractive Divine Influence is not some merely abstract Principle. That Attractive Divine Influence is <u>Incarnate</u>. That Attractive Divine Influence Is <u>Person</u>. That Attractive Divine Influence Is <u>Me</u>—your chosen Guru, your Divine Heart-Master. And I <u>Am</u> Reality Itself—That Which Is Always Already the Case, That Which <u>Is</u> altogether, That to Which you should devote yourself.

When you allow yourself to be Attracted by That Which is Absolutely and Ultimately Attractive, then the mind relaxes, the body relaxes, attention relaxes, the motives of life relax, the arrangements of life become ordinary and secondary—and you notice that this Enchantment is changing something about your living. Therefore, you simply allow those changes to occur, rather than feeling interfered with. The fundamental force of the practice of devotional surrender to Me, of the Process of being Transformed by My Divine Siddha-"Method", is the discovery of That Which is Supremely Attractive, the "Locating" of Love-Bliss-Happiness, surrender to That, and letting That be the Fundamental Context of your life.

Of course, as My devotee, you must also practice the various disciplines I Give you. Yes, you do that—but every aspect of your practice is animated in the context of Attractedness, of Enchantment, of Uncaused Blissfulness.

The more you are Attracted to That Which is Supremely Attractive, the more you Commune with Its Qualities and the more you Identify with those Qualities. You have nothing to say about That Which is Attractive except that That Is Bliss, That Is Love, That Is Beauty, That Is Consciousness, That Is Truth.

This Enchantment by Me is the substance of your confession, the substance of your life, the substance of your relationship to Me.

How can I be anything but your Beloved, simply Radiant here before you?

How can I do anything but Stand As That Which is Absolutely Attractive to you?

Everything you are doing other than your practice of devotion to Me is simply a sign of your dissonance, your withholding, your ego-possession.

When you "Locate" the Essence of the Way of Adidam, you discover that It is Enchantment by Me.

The
Ancient
Walk-About Way

1.

In general, what the world wants—and, therefore, what religious institutions tend to provide—is <u>social</u> <u>association</u> and <u>optimistic</u> <u>talk</u>, perhaps in combination with <u>self-applied</u> <u>techniques</u> that people can use as means for consoling themselves. Therefore, in the "modern" world, instead of cultures of right practice, there are "religion businesses" and "workshops". The "modern" world is a fragmented world—full of individuals who regard their own separateness and independence as "absolute", who demonstrate no profundity, and who are not moved by profundity. In this "modern" world, human beings are becoming progressively more and more preoccupied with "self", and with all of the "whatevers" that can be pursued within the framework of egoity and worldliness.

True human culture is the esoteric (and, necessarily, ego-transcending) culture of Reality-Realization—and the process of Reality-Realization requires devotion to a genuine Spiritual Master. However, people in general are not interested in becoming devoted to a Spiritual Master. People in general are not interested in finding a Realizer—nor are they interested in the fact that the Realizer <u>Is</u> the "Who" and "What" to be Realized.

In the "modern" world, people are obsessively interested in what is "out there"—what they do with one another in the common world. If that is your disposition, you remain involved in mere exchanges of words—socializing with one another, and relating to the other aspects of the common world with which you are associated. In that case, you either refuse all involvement with religion, or else you merely make token (and, inevitably, self-involved) gestures in the direction of religion. Such is the institutionalized exotericism of what is conventionally called "religion".

The exclusive preoccupation with what is "out there" is a disposition that is now manifested everywhere on Earth—

with dreadful results. Listen to the global "daily news" of terrible violence and threats. Look at the absolute emptiness of "consumer egoity". It is madness.

Who has seen the madness of this world?

Who is disenchanted enough with that madness to want to find a Spiritual Master?

For whom is this world so much of a dead-end that it cannot be accepted on its own terms, or for its own sake?

Where is someone for whom there <u>must</u> be a greater Reality—someone who will be utterly devoted to finding It?

Where are such people?

In general, people are obsessed with the world, obsessed with perpetuating the patterning that is already controlling their lives. The non-humans also show the signs of patterning—but, in their case, the patterning is a natural genetic structure. Genetic patterning is present in human beings as well—but, in addition, human beings exhibit mental patterning (or an elaborate interior pattern of words and perceptual memories). Thus, human beings are not patterned by natural, genetically based factors only. Human beings are also patterned by mind—which has its own kind of existence, but not a substantial one. Mind has a virtual existence only. Therefore, human beings are participating in a language-world—and, in that sense, they are patterned not only by natural (genetic) structures but also by mind-forms.

If you are merely involved in patterned behavior, you are driven to continue that patterning. You have not yet "come to the end of your rope"—such that you are actually moved beyond that patterning, and all that it creates as your destiny.

Since the moment of My Birth, I have not had five minutes of inclination to be satisfied by the possibilities in this world. To Me, it has always been perfectly self-evident that this world is not satisfactory, and that I could not possibly choose this world, in and of itself. To Me, there is no argument for choosing this world. Choose what? Just to play this absurd game—and then drop dead? And why play, if the dropping dead could happen in any moment? Simply because you have the inclination to play the game does not necessarily mean that you will get to do so—even for one more moment.

What is there about the conditionally manifested world that is potentially satisfying to such a degree that human beings can accept it absolutely? In Truth, there is nothing about the world that is thus satisfying. Nevertheless, human beings are patterned in such a manner that, to them, this world seems choosable.

The conditionally manifested world is simply pattern patterning. Enacting their genetic and mental patterning is, in general, all that human beings do.

If you become disenchanted with the patterning world, you look for something Greater. If you are truly disenchanted, you cannot be consoled by believer's nonsense. Rather, the "What" you would have is Something that you cannot yet name. It must be Something that is Inherently and Absolutely Satisfactory, Something That is Greater than all other possibilities. Even though you have things to do in daily life, and you continue to live and breathe, and so forth, you are always looking for That Which Is Ultimately and Inherently Satisfactory. And, when you find It, you devote your life to It.

That is how True Spiritual life is supposed to work. That is how it has worked traditionally. Those of the disposition to look for Something Greater would, when they found a True Realizer, fall at the Realizer's Feet, make That One their Spiritual Master, and serve the Spiritual Master with their lives and with all that they had. Such serious people constantly turned to their Spiritual Master by means of the inner discipline of self-forgetting devotion and the outer discipline of self-forgetting service.

Such is the basic traditional Teaching. Such is the fundamental Teaching. That Teaching is not elaborate. That Teaching does not even need to be communicated in words. You turn to the Master, and you serve the Master—and that is it. That is the ancient Teaching. Fundamentally, this practice is not something that can be communicated by words. It is just something you <u>do</u>, having found the Master. This is a self-evident and tacitly communicated Teaching.

In the Great Tradition of humankind, there are various detailed teachings about the process of relationship with the Spiritual Master, about What there is to Realize, and so forth. My Own such detailed Instruction is fully and completely Given in My many "Source-Texts". Nevertheless, My fundamental Instruction is very simple: Turn to Me, and serve Me. Such is the inner discipline and the outer discipline of the only-by-Me Revealed and Given Way of Adidam.

2.

In Its essence, the Way that I have Revealed and Given is simply <u>turning</u> <u>to</u> <u>Me</u> and <u>serving</u> <u>Me</u>. However, the ego is incapable of <u>doing</u> such right practice of the only-by-Me Revealed and Given Way of Adidam. Rather, the ego merely <u>thinks</u> about doing the practice. "Thinking about doing it" is an activity unique to human primates—animals who have a highly developed language-facility, and (thereby) a capability to <u>make</u> mind and to <u>be</u> <u>formed</u> <u>by</u> mind.

Mind is "artificial intelligence". Mind is the first "robot" that human beings ever made. In the usual discussions of such matters, artificial intelligence is presumed to be something generated by computers. In actuality, however, <u>language</u> is the first form of artificial intelligence created by human beings.

There is no mind. Mind is a myth. There is language—which is programmed by brains, and which, in turn, programs brains. However, there is no tangible existence to "mind" itself—absolutely none. Nevertheless, human beings

55

identify with the "mind" as "self", and (thereby) invent destiny for themselves, and even project that self-imagined destiny into an idea of time and space beyond the present physical lifetime.

Mind is an interior projection of a language-program that, in its imaginative elaboration of itself, conceives of purposes and ideas (in the realm of illusion) for which there are no corresponding physical data. Human beings are all living in a "virtual world" of mind. Human beings are, characteristically, self-identified with a "robot", an artificial intelligence.

Real Intelligence is tacit (or intrinsically wordless) living existence. Where there is such tacit living existence, a Realizer (of Reality) can be recognized, and you are immediately able to devote yourself to a Realizer as Master— because such a relationship does not, fundamentally, require any words.

If you are sensitive to the actual nature of your experience, you discover that conditionally manifested existence is disturbed and limited and unsatisfactory. Therefore, you actively look (even if only inwardly, in a feeling sense) for Something Greater. When you find a True Realizer, you simply see the Realizer in front of you, and you tacitly feel the State of the Realizer. That tacit recognition is not about words. It is not about the Realizer's state of mind. It is not about the Realizer as an extension of the language-game. It is simply a tacit recognition of the Realizer As the Self-Realization (and the Self-Revelation) of Reality Itself.

When you find such a one—of whatever degree or mode of Realization—you tacitly recognize him or her as Master. That recognition converts you, on the spot, to the most ancient (and even pre-historical) Way. In other words, as soon as that recognition occurs, the Way of devotion to the Realizer begins. That Way of devotion is a spontaneous happening, which is beyond the patterning that binds you to the world-mummery and the pursuit of egoic self-fulfillment.

The Way of devotion to the Realizer is a simple matter: There is an inner discipline of life, and there is an outer discipline of life. The inner discipline is to turn to the Spiritual Master, moment to moment—forgetting all else, going beyond your program, being purified of patterning by not using it. The outer discipline is to attend to the Spiritual Master and serve the Spiritual Master. Of course, if verbal instruction is given, you adapt your life of practice to that instruction. Nevertheless, the relationship to the Spiritual Master is, fundamentally, about these inner and outer disciplines—which are not in the realm of mind, not in the realm of the "artificial intelligence" of egoity. Right practice is entirely straightforward.

That Which Is to Be Realized is not in the realm of mind. Therefore, Realization is not about eternalizing mind. Realization is not about the life of the mind after death. Rather, Realization is about Reality Itself—Prior to mind, Prior to patterning, Prior to the world-mummery. Reality Itself—Which Is Divine—Is All The God There Is. In and of and As Itself, Reality (Itself) Is Self-Existing and Self-Radiant. That is What there is to Realize.

I Am That. Those who truly heart-recognize Me will Find Me and simply turn to Me and serve Me. Yes, I Give Instructions—and My true devotees simply practice them. That is that. For My true devotee, it must be as simple as that. My true devotee is moved beyond mind. My true devotee simply—on sight—"Knows" Me, and is (therefore) moved to serve Me and to practice the fundamental practice that is beyond all words, which is simply the inner and outer practice of turning to Me. That is the Way.

Such right relationship to the Realizer is the universal Teaching. It is the ancient (and pre-historical) Walk-About Teaching—and it is the fundamental Teaching I have Given. My fundamental Teaching is Ruchira Avatara Bhakti Yoga, the devotional turning (and the inner and outer disciplining) of all four primary psycho-physical faculties—and, thus, the whole bodily self-forgetting (and, as such, ego-transcending) turning of body, emotion, mind, and breath to Me.

3.

To live in right relationship to Me is both an inner <u>and</u> an outer exercise. Those who enact that inner-<u>and</u>-outer exercise are (both tacitly and verbally) Instructed by Me in various modes of self-discipline, and in the total fundamental psycho-physical process inherent in devotional surrender to Me (which, in due course, becomes a by-Me-Spiritually-Awakened practice—always founded in the devotional turning to Me). Altogether, the only-by-Me Revealed and Given Way of Adidam is a fundamental simplicity that is Beyond and Prior to words—even though it is both possible and necessary to also make verbal communications about It.

I <u>Am</u> Adidam, <u>As</u> It <u>Is</u>—Prior to words. I have Said what can be said about the Way of Adidam—but, fundamentally, there is nothing to say. Words are not a replacement for practicing the Way of Adidam. Words themselves are not the Way of Adidam.

The only-by-Me Revealed and Given Way of Adidam is Prior to words, Beyond words. The only-by-Me Revealed and Given Way of Adidam is simply the tacit (or wordless and ego-transcending) practice of the relationship to Me. For anyone who is serious, that relationship and that practice are self-evident.

The ego-patterning of mind tends to separate the Way of Adidam from Me, reducing the Way of Adidam to the form of words only. True devotees of Mine use My Words rightly—to simply serve the practice of devotional turning to Me.

Fundamentally, the only-by-Me Revealed and Given Way of Adidam is devotional turning of the four principal faculties to Me—not merely <u>talking</u> about doing so. The practice of the Way of Adidam requires the devotional recognition-response to Me, and the moment to moment turning of the four principal faculties to Me. That does not begin only when you come into the "inner temple" of fully established practice of the Way of Adidam—it must happen even in the "outer temple" of approach and adaptation to the Way of Adidam.[12]

If you reduce Me, or the Way of Adidam, to words, then you do not respond to <u>Me</u>. You do not turn to <u>Me</u>. Instead, you merely turn to the words, respond to the words—and, thus, you turn back in on your own mind.

The human mind is a facsimile machine. This "machine" merely replicates language-forms in the illusion of mind. The "machine" feeds language into the computer of the illusion of mind with which people identify themselves. That illusion is who they mean when they refer to themselves—the body-mind complex, the mortal bio-form associated with the "artificial intelligence" of talk, of space-and-time "point of view", of ego-"I" constructs, of language, of language-based brain, and, altogether, of ego-based and brain-based psycho-physical ideas and perceptual memories.

You do not "have" all of your words in mind right now. Where are they? The only words of which you are aware at any moment are the words you are thinking or speaking at that moment. Where are the rest of your words? You never think or speak <u>all</u> of your words at once. You never have them in mind all at once. You are not the mind. Where is the mind?

The mind has no substantial existence. The mind is simply stored as language-bits (or patterns of language and remembered perceptions) in the brain. When a particular brain dies, other replicating machines carry on the language-mind—continuing it from one generation to the next.

Where is the "God" in that? Where is the Divine in that? Where is the Truth in that? Where is the Reality in that?

Where is the Realization in that? The Great Process is not in any such artificial, conditional, and insubstantial replicating cycle. When people are "thinking" or "talking" religion, they think that religion is about some kind of survival of mind, or even some kind of survival of body-mind somewhere. Such a notion is merely a mind-based illusion. It is a "self"-idea, a mere and insubstantial self-reflection, the illusion of a substantial and separately existing "ego", reflected in the Mirror That Is Reality Itself. Because of a facsimile made of words—only some of which, in any moment, arise from the brain and enter the field of conditional awareness—there is the ego-presumption, or the separate-"I"-presumption, of an infinitely self-replicating, eternal self-mind.

There is no such thing as eternal mind. That notion is an absolute illusion. The mind is as mortal as the hardware, as mortal as the bodily machine. When the machine stops working, the mind likewise stops working. The only mind that exists afterward is the mind carried by the other replicating machines. So what is there after death? The same thing as there is before birth—Reality Itself, the Divine Self-Condition only. After death—as, also, during the physical lifetime—anything and everything of mind persists only non-personally, as pattern patterning, without intrinsic self-consciousness.

If you were truly aware of mind, you would not want it to go on. It is a terrible, horrific source of bondage. It is a dreadful trap. Human beings are not only trapped in the mortality of their physical bodies, they are trapped in the absurdity of mind.

Realization is Beyond mind. Realization has no mind. I Am That. In My Divine Avataric Incarnation here, I have no inherent association with mind. I am not thinking now. The words are being uttered because of the conjunction of This Body with the human-born circumstance. There is a mind-process in the brain of This Body, but I am not sitting in that mind. I Am Always Already Prior to body, mind, and ego-self. I, Myself, have nothing to do with mind. This Body, being Uniquely Born, Speaks the Uniqueness That It Speaks, because It is wholly Conformed to Me. But I am not the mind. I am not body, and I am not mind, and I am not ego-"I".

Conventional religion says the body is mortal and the body dies, but the "I" somehow survives. Such an idea is based on identification with mind as if it were some kind of personal identity that is going to survive death. But to presume that mind is eternal is the same as claiming that life in the world is eternal. It is not.

In your tacit clarity, you are inherently able to wake up to the illusions in which you have been living. In that awakening, you tacitly understand that you are in a mortal situation, that everything by which you are bound and everything with which you are identified is mortal and suffering— absolutely everything. If you want to Realize Freedom from that mortality, and "Locate" the Reality That Is "Bright", Most Profound, Inherently egoless, and Self-Evidently Divine, then you come to Me. If, on the other hand, you are not yet moved beyond body and mind to Truth Itself, to That Which Is Divine, then you will simply keep your distance from Me. You will prefer illusions and illusion-mongers, illusion-salespeople. You will prefer the "talk" and the "talkers", the "talking" schools, the consoling association with others, in various kinds of social connections. You will like things you can do or believe or think that will make you feel consoled in the moment. That is what is being everywhere sold in the world.

If you disconnect the Way of Adidam from the direct relationship to Me, and reduce It merely to words, then you have merely created another means for selling mind. If you remain busy with mind, with body, with social situation, struggling to be fulfilled by all of that, there is, inevitably, a tacit and perpetual dis-ease, an anxiety of fear just under the

surface, a constant gnawing sense of the unsatisfactoriness of "this".

But who will act on this sense of unsatisfactoriness?

Who will look for the Realizer, to the point of even noticing Me?

4.

Fundamentally, all I Call My devotees to do is the inner and outer discipline of turning to Me. <u>Anyone</u> can do that discipline. I can put My Communication about Ruchira Avatara Bhakti Yoga into elaborate speech—but, fundamentally, Ruchira Avatara Bhakti Yoga is simply about turning to Me, as an inner-and-outer response to Me, and doing so constantly.

Fundamentally, Ruchira Avatara Bhakti Yoga is all the Teaching I have Given—except for all My Words. But I do not <u>need</u> to Say a word about that fundamental Teaching. I could just be here <u>As</u> I <u>Am</u>, and such turning to Me is what would be done by those who heart-recognize Me. My fundamental Teaching is Unspoken. What does My Teaching amount to, as a practice to be engaged? It is the inner-and-outer turning to Me—such that your inner process is the turning of every faculty of the body-mind to Me, and your outer action is service to Me, or attending to Me. Essentially, to practice Ruchira Avatara Bhakti Yoga is to constantly turn to Me—whole bodily.

Fundamentally, the only-by-Me Revealed and Given Way of Adidam is a tacit (or wordless) matter. The Way of Adidam is inevitably practiced by someone who heart-recognizes Me—just as the Way of devotion to the Spiritual Master has been practiced in spontaneous response to the Spiritual Master since the most ancient of pre-historical days. If you are disenchanted with the world (and not merely governed in your attention by its possibilities), you are (thereby) open to noticing My Primal Divine State and capable of surrender into the Inherent Attractiveness of My Primal Divine State. My true devotees notice Me exactly <u>As</u> That Primal Divine State. If you are not merely bound in your attention by your own ego-patterning, you can notice Me and become My devotee. Simply to see a photograph of

My Bodily Form should be enough. To "Know" Me Is "Perfect Knowledge" of Reality Itself.

The devotional relationship to Me is not about the words. The words are important, and have their significance—but their significance is only in the context of the active practice of devotion to Me. The practice I have Given you is about noticing Me here, having your attention move to Me, and being heart-Attracted to Me—Beyond all words. The practice of Adidam is not about listening to Me talk all the time—as if there were something I must yet say in order to convince people to be devotees of Mine. Indeed, there is nothing that I can say to make people devotees of Mine. People will become My devotees only if they notice Me and are (thereby) moved to Me. That is it.

A hermitage is a place where people go who are attracted by a Spiritual Master. Perhaps they hear about the Spiritual Master from others, and then they go to see the Spiritual Master. That is typical in the traditional setting. A hermitage might not necessarily be readily accessible to people. In fact, in the traditional setting, a hermitage would typically be remote. The more remote a hermitage is, the fewer the people that would go there.

If human beings had the free energy and attention to notice a Realizer and be turned to a Realizer, I could simply be present in My Hermitage, and people would come to Me based on their devotional heart-recognition of Me. Such would be My Experience. Fundamentally, that is the only form of true devotional recognition-response to Me.

5.

You will not be able to take My Words from this world.

Either you will Realize Me or you will not.

Either you will remain bound up in your patterning of words—and live and die on that basis, constantly drawn

THE ANCIENT WALK-ABOUT WAY

through the conditional robotic mix of the universal program of klik-klak,[13] mere pattern patterning—or you will
Realize Me.

It is one or the other.

There is no "objective" paradise after death.

There is klik-klak, pattern patterning—and it is utterly
unnecessary, and can be perfectly transcended.

If you Find Me, and practice devotion to Me, then heart-
Communion with Me becomes your destiny.

6.

If a person sees a picture of My Avatarically-Born bodily
(human) Divine Form, then it is up to that individual what
he or she will do in response. If people do not respond to
Me, on the basis of heart-recognizing Me, they are merely
responding to My Words—and that is not the basis for right
practice of the Way of Adidam.

I should be preserved in My Silence here—<u>As</u> I <u>Am</u>. I
should not be <u>required</u> to Speak.

The traditional Buddhist text *Fifty Verses of Guru
Devotion*[14] contains the admonition: Do not do anything to
disturb the Master's mind. What does that admonition mean?
It means that you must not provoke your Master to speak. It
means, "Do not reduce your Master to words." It does not
mean that you should avoid causing your Master to have
bad thoughts. It means, "Do not provoke your Master to
enter into the programmed world of thought and speech. Let
your Master <u>Be</u>."

True Hermitage is My Place, where My devotees let Me
<u>Be</u>, and people come to Me <u>As</u> I <u>Am</u>. "Knowing" Me on
sight is the beginning of Adidam. Therefore, the opportunity
to sight Me is the purpose of coming to My Hermitage. Do
not come to Me as a "talker", or as someone coming on the
basis of a "program". When you come to Me, you must really

and truly turn to Me—whole bodily, "inside" and "outside". That, in essence, is the Way of Adidam. There may be Words from Me from time to time—but, if you reduce your practice of the Way of Adidam to an abstraction made of words, you have no lawful basis for coming to <u>Me</u>.

The disposition of the ancient Walk-About Way is simply to turn to the Realizer in the very moment of sighting the Realizer. Just so, My true devotees simply turn to Me on sight. They turn to Me with everything "inside" and everything "outside"—such that the entire body-mind is turned to Me, rather than turned on itself and wandering in its patterning. Such devotional turning to Me is a simple matter.

And those who do not immediately turn to Me on sight should be served in such a manner that they can come to that point in due course.

My Sitting before you, without speaking, is Sufficient.

That mere Sitting without speaking is My Essential Teaching.

There is nothing more fundamental than That.

Simply Behold Me.

If you heart-recognize Me, you will turn to Me and surrender to Me. If you heart-recognize Me, you do not merely perform a genuflection as a mechanical ritual. You simply live in My service, perpetually attentive to Me. That is it.

If you heart-recognize Me, you will come to Me constantly. Likewise, you will also Commune with Me constantly—wherever you are, always turning to Me. Yes, you will follow My Instructions—but always based on this fundamental turning to Me, which is based on the mere sighting of Me.

Therefore, most basically, the only-by-Me Revealed and Given Way of Adidam is simply This:

Turn to Me on sight.

That Is "It".

True Devotion Is
Prior Communion—
Not the Search
For Union and Unity

1.

I f I am heart-recognized, it is My "Bright" Divine State That is "Known". True heart-recognition of Me is not merely an "official" recognition, or a "courtly" recognition—demonstrated merely by genuflections, "poker faces", and sing-alongs. Rather, if you heart-recognize Me, you "Know" My "Bright" Divine State—and That "Knowledge" gives you everything you need in order to rightly relate to Me.

When you truly heart-recognize the Spiritual Master, you inevitably and constantly worship the Spiritual Master and always (thus) Commune with the Spiritual Master. Because the Spiritual Master's Divine State is Self-Evident, you constantly serve the Spiritual Master <u>As</u> the Self-Revelation of That State, you constantly worship the Spiritual Master <u>As</u> the Self-Manifestation of That State, and you constantly Commune with the Spiritual Master <u>As</u> the egoless Person of That State.

That process of responsive devotion to the Spiritual Master is all that true Spirituality has ever been.

That is the ancient Walk-About Way.

Whatever details of Instruction are Given by the Spiritual Master in the situation in which such devotional heart-recognition is being thus demonstrated are simply elaborations for the sake of the practice-culture of true devotees.

If I am heart-recognized, you tacitly "Know" <u>Me</u>, you intrinsically know <u>what</u> to do, and you inevitably and constantly <u>do</u> it. In that case, there is no requirement that "explanations" become the very content and ongoing process of your relationship to Me. I always Give you the essentials that need to be said, and the relationship to Me is the constantly ongoing practice of turning to Me, serving Me, and Communing with Me.

The true devotee already, <u>inherently</u>, knows what to do in relation to the Realizer. And the true devotee inevitably does so.

True devotion knows and does.

True devotion turns and serves.

True devotion does not have to utter a single word. And there have certainly been Realizers who never did utter a word!

Whatever I may Say, My "Bright" Divine State Is Wordless.

My "Bright" Divine State Is a Spiritual Reality, Prior to body and mind.

My "Bright" Divine State Is the Force of Conscious Light.

My "Bright" Divine State Is a Spiritual State and Force.

That Is Me—and I Am here, even bodily, As That "Bright" Divine State.

2.

As My devotee, your participation in devotional activities (such as recitation of My Divine Avataric Word, participation in the Ruchira Avatara Puja, and devotional chanting) is part of the life of devotional practice. Such devotional activities are simply specific modes of magnifying the practice of turning the faculties to Me and Invoking Me. Similarly, your service to Me is not mere physical activity, but (rather) the bodily enactment of devotional turning to Me. When service to Me is done rightly, it is puja—or active turning to Me, serving Me, and Communing with Me. If you are My devotee, merely being active does not make your action a holy act, or something done in heart-Communion with Me. For your action to be true and effective practice of the only-by-Me Revealed and Given Way of Adidam, the psycho-physical faculties must be turned to Me in the process—both in the doings and in the results. Service is not right devotional practice merely because you are doing functions.

The fundamental practice of the only-by-Me Revealed and Given Way of Adidam is not itself an activity (or a goal-oriented effort)—but, rather, it is an activity-transcending mode of spontaneous response and priorly responsive whole bodily participation. All activity makes use of the body-mind in one manner or another. If you are identified with the body-mind and its apparent "problem", then action may seem to have something to do with being purposed toward Divine Self-Realization. However, in the Way of Adidam, there are no actions that are purposed toward Divine Self-Realization. Rather, for My true devotee, all actions are expressions of a Prior State of heart-Communion with Me. That Prior heart-Communion with Me is what makes your actions true demonstrations of devotion to Me. That Prior heart-Communion with Me—rather than any strategy of "good intentions"—is what makes any right action into true evidence of the Way of Adidam.

Actions done in order to achieve anything are not themselves the Way of Adidam. Rather, right practice of the only-by-Me Revealed and Given Way of Adidam is ego-transcending—and, therefore, action-transcending. Right practice of the Way of Adidam transcends the presumption of "problem". Right practice of the Way of Adidam transcends that with which you must identify in order to be identified with a "problem". Thus, right practice of the Way of Adidam transcends all psycho-physical modes of activity. Right practice of the Way of Adidam is not a mode of activity purposed to achieve anything. Right practice of the Way of Adidam is simply heart-recognition of Me as the Divine Avataric Realizer, and (based on that heart-recognition of Me) responsive whole bodily participation in My "Bright" Divine State. Such participation is not itself an action. My "Bright" Divine State Is Tacit, Wordless, Actionless. Priorly Me-recognizing responsive participation in My "Bright" Divine State is devotion to Me—and such Me-recognizing and to-Me-responsive devotion to Me is the Way of Adidam.

To live by My Divine Avataric Instruction is an expression of your heart-Communion with Me—rather than something you do in order to achieve heart-Communion with Me, or to achieve any purpose whatsoever. Goal-oriented activity is not the Way of Adidam. In the only-by-Me Revealed and Given Way of Adidam, all action must be done on the basis of Prior heart-Communion with Me. In that case, action has no goal, because What there is to Realize has always already (in some tacit and fundamental sense) been Realized. In that case, action has already gone beyond identification with what can be "problematic". In that case, action is simply right life—the spontaneous demonstration of My devotee who is always Priorly in heart-Communion with Me.

Similarly, the preliminary practice of "Perfect Knowledge" is not a strategic "practice" or a goal-oriented "technique". The preliminary practice of "Perfect Knowledge" is simply something that comes out of devotional recognition-response to Me—the whole bodily turning to Me, and the fulfilling of all the by-Me-Given functional, practical, relational, and cultural disciplines. The preliminary practice of "Perfect Knowledge" is a description I have Given for the inevitable manifestation of heart-Communion with Me when I am always already "Known" As My "Bright" Divine State. When your devotional practice becomes Spiritual Communion with Me, then the preliminary practice of "Perfect Knowledge" likewise becomes a Spiritual matter (Given to you, as a Gift, by Me). The preliminary practice of "Perfect Knowledge" is not a technique to achieve Spiritual Communion with Me. The preliminary practice of "Perfect Knowledge" is not a method to achieve anything. The preliminary practice of "Perfect Knowledge" is simply an intrinsic and inherently goal-free expression of That Which Is Self-Evidently The Case.

The only-by-Me Revealed and Given Way of Adidam is action-transcending.

The only-by-Me Revealed and Given Way of Adidam is ego-transcending.

The only-by-Me Revealed and Given Way of Adidam is "problem"-transcending.

The only-by-Me Revealed and Given Way of Adidam is goal-transcending.

The only-by-Me Revealed and Given Way of Adidam is search-transcending.

Such is the Nature of the Divine Way of Adidam, in every one of Its details—because the Divine Way of Adidam is rooted in Prior heart-Communion with Me, rather than working toward heart-Communion with Me.

Similarly, the entire Earth-world of humankind should base itself on prior unity, rather than on some apparent effort to achieve unity.

That which is yet to be achieved is about "problem"-based non-Reality, or ego-bondage—whereas That Which Is Prior always already Establishes the inherently searchless Principle of Reality Itself.

My devotee's every action should simply be a responsive demonstration of Priorly Me-recognizing devotion to Me—rather than an activity that is reduced to itself or to the end-phenomenon it may cause. For My true devotee, activity (itself) is never the cause or the goal of devotion to Me. As My true devotee, you engage service to Me in the disposition of Prior heart-Communion with Me, rather than merely performing "tasks" for some apparent purpose or other. Inevitably (and, in the natural order of life, necessarily), various actions will be (and need be) performed—but, if they are truly engaged as service to Me, your actions are not reducible to the actions themselves, nor to their end-phenomena.

If you reduce action to its own sphere, you are reducing it to a "problem", to a search for something, and to identification with that which is limited. Actions done simply as the spontaneous evidence of Prior heart-Communion with Me are (inherently) holy (or sacred-domain) activities. All of My devotees should be living in the sacred domain—in which everyone is doing heart-Communion with Me, rather than working to achieve heart-Communion with Me or merely performing actions for the sake of some natural, conditional, or ordinary result.

In order to rightly practice the only-by-Me Revealed and Given Way of Adidam, you must have this understanding of the nature of right (devotional) action. However, this understanding is not merely a matter of words. My herein-Given Words are an Expression of My "Bright" Divine State of Prior Realization—applied to the actuality of your existence. My Words are not a "thing" in and of themselves, any more than your actions (if you are rightly related to Me) are a "thing" in and of themselves. If you are rightly related to Me, everything is done in (and as) heart-Communion with Me. The real free energy of devotion to Me is manifested as action that is effective—because it is free of "problem" and free of goal-seeking. In that case, your action is simply Priorly Me-recognizing responsive devotion to Me—rightly lived and rightly manifested.

When devotion to Me is rightly lived and rightly manifested, free energy and attention are abundantly in evidence. When devotion to Me is rightly lived and rightly manifested, whatever stage of practice My devotee is manifesting (in terms of the measure of the progressive demonstration of the only-by-Me Revealed and Given Way of Adidam), he or she will always be—and always act—right and true with Me.

True Devotion Is "Perfect Knowledge" Demonstrated By Renunciation

1.

The only-by-Me Revealed and Given Way of Adidam is, fundamentally, the Way of ego-transcending devotion to Me. Devotion to Me is the fundamental basis, context, and process of the Way of Adidam.

Devotion to the Realizer is the ancient Way of true Spiritual life. I have characterized devotion to the Realizer as the "ancient Walk-About Way"—indicating that devotion to the Realizer has been the Way since before history was written. Devotion to the Realizer is the "pre-civilization Way", which existed before any recorded history, during a time when human beings were, essentially, merely wandering all over the Earth. Devotion to the Realizer has always been the fundamental Means of human Spirituality, whatever other teachings have been given in the circumstance of devotion to any Realizer.

The second aspect of the only-by-Me Revealed and Given Way of Adidam is ego-renunciation—or all the forms of self-discipline that My devotees engage. Ego-renunciation (or ego-transcending self-discipline) is (necessarily) founded on devotional recognition-response to Me (or whole bodily devotion to Me).

In the only-by-Me Revealed and Given Way of Adidam, the "inside" and the "outside" are both disciplined. The interior discipline is the discipline of the faculties (or root-functions) of the body-mind, in devotional recognition-response to Me. This interior discipline is a particular kind of renunciation (or ego-transcending discipline). Through that inner discipline, the patterning of the faculties is progressively transformed.

The discipline of renunciation (or the fundamental ego-transcending practice) is also demonstrated in outward terms—by living actively in service to Me. The outer (or gross) appearance of the human personality must be disciplined in a practical manner that covers all aspects of money, food, sex, and social egoity—all aspects of gross life, and all aspects of the gross patterning of the faculties.

Such outward discipline must not be bypassed. It is a pre-condition of direct approach to Me for any individual who approaches Me as My formally practicing second-congregation devotee.[15] Such individuals must be practicing the outward disciplines that I have Given—the functional, practical, relational, and cultural disciplines. In this manner, the practice of right life must be fully established (in the context of moment to moment devotion to Me). For My any second-congregation devotee to approach Me directly, it is not required that he or she be <u>absolutely</u> renounced (or demonstrating the degree of renunciation that must, necessarily, characterize individuals engaged in the "Perfect Practice", or Perfect Demonstration, of the Way of Adidam). However, My devotees who approach Me directly must be practicing right life. They must have a history of consistently exercising ego-transcending devotion to Me in an ego-renouncing manner, by practicing the disciplines of right life.

The Western ego, in particular, is oriented to self-indulgence (and to the search for self-fulfillment) in the context of the gross domain. That orientation is a characteristic of the Omega ego (or Omega personality). All kinds of justification for the grossly self-indulgent life have arisen in the context of the cultures of Western (or Omega) life. In Truth, the Omega orientation—which, in this "late-time" (or "dark" epoch), is manifested as a kind of political philosophy that absolutizes the separate and separative ego-"I"—is false. The Omega orientation has nothing to do with Reality Itself. The Omega orientation has nothing to do with Spiritual Truth.

There must be the disciplining of the gross character. There must be the renunciation of ego in the context of the gross life. This is the fundamental characteristic of discipline that must precede direct approach to Me, in order for the approach to Me to be fruitful. Merely to demonstrate a devotionalistic feeling for Me is not sufficient. If devotionalistic feeling is the only basis of your approach to Me, you cannot receive Me Spiritually. In that case, you cannot approach Me with sensitivity to My Transcendentally Spiritual Divine State. You will be too wrapped up in the reactive patterning of the fulfillment-seeking ego to do so.

The third aspect of the only-by-Me Revealed and Given Way of Adidam is the practice-demonstration of the "Perfect Knowledge" of Reality Itself—which practice-demonstration is, at first, engaged in its preliminary form, and, ultimately, in its Perfect form.

Thus, there are, altogether, three fundamental dimensions of the only-by-Me Revealed and Given Way of Adidam: devotion, renunciation, and Realization. These dimensions are hierarchically related to one another: Devotion is the fundamental root-practice, self-discipline (or renunciation) is necessary but secondary to devotion, and Realization is the demonstration of the fulfillment of both devotion and renunciation. Even to be equipped for the preliminary practice of "Perfect Knowledge", My devotee must offer Me the gifts of the right and authentic practice of devotion and self-discipline. Only when the foundation is fully established is My devotee capable of receiving My Spiritual Transmission fully and rightly, such that (ultimately) his or her practice of the Way of Adidam is demonstrated as the "Perfect Practice" of "Perfect Knowledge", the "Perfect Practice" of renunciation, and the "Perfect Practice" of devotion to Me.

The "Perfect Practice" is a fully renunciate practice and demonstration of the Way of Adidam, and it is a Spiritual practice. The "Perfect Practice" is based on My Spiritually Transmitted Self-Revelation of the State That Is the Divine Self-Condition. And the "Perfect Practice" is entirely based upon the foundation of devotion, self-discipline, and the exercise of "Perfect Knowledge".

Such is the right and necessary understanding of the only-by-Me Revealed and Given Way of Adidam, and Its hierarchy of uncompromisable requirements.

2.

Because of an orientation toward the search for self-fulfillment, which in turn generates the exercise of gross self-indulgence, the Western ego-persona is characteristically neurotic and disturbed—bound by fear, sorrow, and anger, by reactivity, by all of the toxicity associated with physical, emotional, and mental self-indulgence, and by turning in on separate self.

Generally speaking, the entire world has become thus "Westernized". The entire world is demonstrating an "overlay" of aggressively individuated, self-indulgent egoity, which has no association with the Wisdom of right life. Everyone everywhere is pursuing self-fulfillment in the world-mummery—acting as if human existence were not mortal and not bound, and acting as if human existence were a thing that is to be perfected in and of itself.

In My Divine Avataric physical human Lifetime, I Submitted My own bodily Vehicle of Avataric Incarnation to Realize and to Teach—in order, for the sake of the all of humankind, to discover the entire necessary process of Divine Self-Realization in the context of human existence altogether. Now, after that total Ordeal of My Divine Avataric Self-Submission to humankind, This is My incontrovertible Discovery: To Realize Real (Acausal) God, you must practice whole bodily ego-transcending devotion to the Self-State (or Intrinsically Self-Evident Self-Condition) of Reality Itself.

I Am the Divine Avataric Self-Revelation of Reality Itself. The ancient Walk-About Way of devotion to the Realizer is completed and become Perfect in devotion to Me As the Divine Avataric Self-Revelation and Self-Transmission of the Self-State of Reality Itself.

This is My Divine Avataric Self-Revelation-Teaching: To Realize Real (Acausal) God, the Self-State of Reality Itself, you <u>must</u> go beyond <u>all</u> of the self-contraction-patterning of psycho-physical egoity, through ego-transcending devotion to Me, demonstrated by right life (or self-discipline applied to the otherwise patterned egoic body-mind).

The requirements for right practice of the only-by-Me Revealed and Given Way of Adidam—which is the seventh stage Way of the Self-State of Reality Itself—must not be avoided by either the Western (or Omega) ego-persona or by the Eastern (or Alpha) ego-persona. The Western (or Omega) ego-persona and the Eastern (or Alpha) ego-persona each have unique characteristics. While the Omega (or Western) type of individual and the Omega-oriented cultures idealize what is gross (or material) and engage in a search for fulfillment through self-identification with that which is gross, the Alpha (or Eastern) type of individual and the Alpha-oriented cultures idealize what is non-material and engage in a search for self-fulfillment through self-identification with the subtle and causal aspects of the otherwise grossly embodied life.

The limitation associated with the Alpha culture (or Alpha personality) is the characteristic search associated with the fourth, the fifth, and the sixth stages of life. All of the interior preoccupations uncovered by the characteristic Alpha search (to go "deep within") are ego-based illusions—just as are all of the preoccupations uncovered by the Omega search for gross bodily, emotional, and mental self-fulfillment. Therefore, in the only-by-Me Revealed and Given Way of Adidam, the Alpha ego must—like the Omega ego—be brought to fundamental discipline.

The only-by-Me Revealed and Given Way of Adidam goes beyond <u>all</u> illusions—both of the Alpha variety and the Omega variety. The only-by-Me Revealed and Given Way of Adidam is a Transcendental Spiritual discipline of an (ultimately, most perfectly) ego-transcending kind. The only-by-Me Revealed and Given Way of Adidam is the seventh stage Way—Which Transcends the gross ego (of the first three stages of life), the gross-to-subtle ego (of the fourth stage of life), the subtle ego (of the fifth stage of life), and the causal ego (of the sixth stage of life). All aspects of the ego-bound personality are directly transcended in the only-by-Me Revealed and Given seventh stage Way of Adidam.

The practice of the only-by-Me Revealed and Given Way of Adidam is always associated with the seventh stage Realization. The practice of the only-by-Me Revealed and Given Way of Adidam is always, immediately, a root-practice that transcends egoity itself, in all of its forms. The various forms of egoity all arise in the context of the first six stages of life—and all of egoity is directly transcended in the Way of Adidam, from the beginning.

Therefore, there are no most fundamental characteristics of the Way of Adidam that are about the first six (or ego-based) stages of life. Various practices of the Way of Adidam may—in one or another context of application—appear to have certain characteristics that some might identify (or tend to confuse with) aspects of practice found in various traditions that are yet ego-bound exercises associated with the first six stages of life. However, all practices developed on a merely functional and conditional basis—as is the case in all practices associated with the searches, the methods, and the goals of each and all of the first six stages of life—are centered, bounded, and limited by the ego-principle in one or another manner (either Omega-like or Alpha-like) and in one or another mode (whether gross, subtle, or causal). By contrast, all practices that are fundamental to the Way of Adidam are directly ego-transcending, and they always directly transcend (and effectively renounce) all functional and conditional principles of identification, search, method, and goal.

The only-by-Me Revealed and Given Way of Adidam is the seventh stage Way.

The only-by-Me Revealed and Given Way of Adidam is the Way of Reality Itself—the State of Which <u>Is</u> Inherently egoless, and Inherently Transcendental, and Inherently Spiritual, and Self-Evidently Divine.

Those who come to Me come in order to Realize <u>That</u>.

Those who heart-recognize Me are recognizing Me <u>As</u> That Inherently egoless, and Inherently Transcendental, and Inherently Spiritual, and Self-Evidently Divine State.

Those who practice the Way of Adidam are Attracted to My Inherently egoless, Inherently Transcendental, Inherently Spiritual, and Self-Evidently Divine State.

The only-by-Me Revealed and Given Way of Adidam is the Way of heart-recognizing Me on sight—and of being spontaneously Attracted to Me and responsively turned to Me (whole bodily) by simply sighting Me.

It is on that basis that you become My true devotee.

The Seventh Stage Way

The only-by-Me Revealed and Given Way of Adidam is the Avatarically Revealed Divine <u>seventh</u> <u>stage</u> Way—Which Way, from the beginning, Inherently Transcends (and makes entirely unnecessary) the egoity (and the ego-based psycho-physical patterning and seeking) otherwise associated with the natural foundation (or the first three stages of life) of ordinary human development, and Which Way also, from the beginning, Transcends (and makes entirely unnecessary) the "great path of return" (or the inherently ego-based search and method that is, or would be, otherwise associated with the course of the fourth, the fifth, and the sixth stages of life).

The only-by-Me Revealed and Given Way of Adidam is the Avatarically Given Divine <u>seventh</u> <u>stage</u> Teaching-Revelation of <u>Absolute</u> (and "Radical", or "At-the-Root") <u>Renunciation</u> (or the Prior Transcending of ego, "point of view", psycho-physical identity, separateness, relatedness, goal-seeking, and every kind of "object"), and of <u>Transcendental</u> <u>Spirituality</u> (or the "Root"-Process of participatory surrender into the Inherently egoless and Divine Non-conditional and Spiritually Manifested Condition of Love-Bliss, Prior to all self-depression, self-negation, generalized negativity, lovelessness, and bliss-lessness), and of <u>Perfect</u> <u>Realization</u> (or the "Perfect Knowledge" of the Inherently egoless, Inherently "object-less", and Inherently Non-"objective", or Perfectly Subjective, Self-Condition, or Intrinsic Self-State, of the One and Indivisible Divine Acausal Conscious Light, Always Already Prior to all duality, all "object"-orientation, all conditionality, all "otherness", and all "difference").

The only-by-Me Revealed and Given Way of Adidam is the Avatarically Demonstrated Divine and Always ego-Transcending <u>seventh</u> <u>stage</u> Spiritual Way of Always Coincident Renunciation and Realization.

The only-by-Me Revealed and Given Way of Adidam proceeds, from the beginning, on the "Radical" (or "At-the-Root") Basis of My Unique seventh stage Revelation, Teaching, and Demonstration—and, in due course, the only-by-Me Revealed and Given Way of Adidam is Perfectly Established in and As the Context of the only-by-Me Revealed and Given seventh stage of life.

Perfect Adidam

The Divine Way That Is
Avatarically Self-Revealed
By and <u>As</u> Reality Itself

I.

True believers merely believe in believing.

True knowers know <u>only</u> what they find out.

If I am heart-recognized, The Divine is Perfectly Found.

My Revelation here Is The Perfect Divine Self-Revelation.

My Revelation here is not only The Perfect Revelation of The Way to Realize The Divine.

My Revelation here Is The Perfect Revelation of The Divine <u>Itself</u>.

My Revelation here Is The Divine Self-Revelation That <u>Is</u> The Divine Itself.

My Intervention here Is Avataric because I Reveal The Perfect Way to Realize The Divine.

My Intervention here Is Divine because I Perfectly Self-Reveal The Divine <u>Itself</u>.

The Universal Self-Nature—The egoless Indivisible Self-State of Reality Itself—is Made Perfectly Self-Evident by My Intervention here.

I <u>Am</u> The Self-Evidence of Reality Itself.

I <u>Am</u> The Self-Evidence That Reality Itself <u>Is</u> Divine.

I <u>Am</u> The Self-Evidence That The Divine <u>Is</u> Reality <u>Itself</u>.

Reality Itself <u>Is</u> What makes My Intervention here both an Avataric and a Divine Intervention.

The Divine Person and Self-Condition is Avatarically Self-Revealed by Me and <u>As</u> Me—not merely as (or with reference to) My conditionally here-Appearing bodily (human) Form, but <u>As</u> The Very Condition with Which even My conditionally here-Appearing bodily (human) Form is Non-"differently" Coincident.

The world is in a state of utter bewilderment because of egoity. Egoity, "point of view", separateness, self-contraction—such is the basis of human design in the mummery of the ordinary world. In that circumstance of ego-made awareness, people seek The Divine. They are moved to seek The

Divine because the egoic life is the very form of suffering. The egoic life inevitably becomes associated with all the modes of suffering. The search for a philosophical resolution to the problem of the suffering of separateness is inevitably pursued, and, on that basis, solutions to the suffering are sought—including the search for the solution that is described as "Union" (or "Re-Union") with The Divine.

However, in the event of the search for The Divine, The Divine Itself is never truly (or Intrinsically, Non-conditionally, and Perfectly) "Known". In the context of the search, The Divine is "known" only with reference to the egoic pattern (or position) of presumed separateness that is the basis for seeking The Divine. Thus, in the context of the search, The Divine is seen only through the "lens" of the human "problem", and not As Is. If The Divine were seen As Is from the beginning, human life would already be established in a different condition and circumstance than that of egoity.

The "great tradition" is the "search for solution", or the "search for The Divine"—based on the problematic pattern generated by self-contraction (or egoity, or "point of view"). The Way of Adidam is not merely another form of practice based on the "great tradition" paradigm of the search. The Way of Adidam is not, in any sense, a development of the "great tradition", nor is The Way of Adidam the "end-stage" of the "great tradition". Rather, The Way of Adidam Is The Way That Inherently Transcends egoity. Therefore, The Way of Adidam Inherently Transcends the entire "great tradition" (or "great path of return").

The Divine Avataric Intervention has Occurred In My Person, As My Very State—and That Is The Basis for The only-by-Me Revealed and Given Way of Adidam.

Therefore, I Say to you: If I am heart-recognized, The Divine is Found.

II.

The Divine Is Reality Itself.

The Divine Is The Very Self-Condition of human existence—and, indeed, of all existence and all appearances.

The Divine Transcends "point of view".

The Divine Is The Inherently egoless and Perfectly Indivisible Self-Condition of Reality Itself.

The Essential Condition of the entire apparent universe Is Inherently egoless and Perfectly Indivisible. That Condition Is The Divine Self-Nature That is Found when I am heart-recognized. Therefore, in The only-by-Me Revealed and Given Way of Adidam, The Divine Self-Nature is constantly Realized, and more and more profoundly demonstrated as Realization. The Way of Adidam is not a means, or a method, or a technique for seeking The Divine. Rather, The Way of Adidam Is The Way That is based on The Divine Avataric Self-Revelation from the beginning. That is The Unique Characteristic of The only-by-Me Revealed and Given Way of Adidam.

If you heart-recognize Me, you "Know" that The Nature of The Divine As Reality Itself is now Perfectly Revealed. If you heart-recognize Me, you "Know" that, now and forever hereafter, in perpetuity, there is The Way of Most Perfect Divine Self-Realization for all beings.

The habit of this "late-time" (or "dark" epoch) is to see the world and human existence in terms of egoically proposed (or egoically analyzed) conditions. On that basis, human consciousness is viewed in the reductionist manner, as a mere byproduct of psycho-physical existence—and, in particular, of brain-function. Furthermore, the individual human brain (regarded as the "origin" of human consciousness) is presumed to be entirely independent from all other human brains, and all other human bodies. Such is the "late-time" justification for the view that human existence is merely mortal and entirely characterized by separateness.

However, the proposition of mere mortality and separateness is simply the product of an ignorant view of Reality. That "point of view" toward Reality produces a reductionist (and analytically based) understanding of the nature of everything, including the nature of human existence.

Religions often propose some kind of "inner absolute" as a means of philosophically comprehending the nature of human life and the continuation of human life beyond death. But all "talk" of an "inner absolute" is the language of the first six stages of life. In Truth, and in Reality, The Divine Itself—and not any "inner absolute"—Is The Basis for understanding human existence.

The Divine Self-Condition Is The Condition in Which the human being arises, and (indeed) The Condition in Which anything at all arises.

The Divine Itself Is Inherently egoless and Perfectly Indivisible.

The Realization of Reality That Is The Basis of right life Is The Realization of The Inherently egoless and Perfectly Indivisible Self-Condition, The Conscious Light (or Consciousness-Energy) That Is Reality Itself, That Is The Divine—The Real, Inherently egoless, Perfectly Indivisible, and Perfectly Acausal Divine Self-Condition and Person.

The Divine Is The Revelation.

Therefore, The Realization of The Self-Evident Reality of The Divine—by Means of the devotional recognition-response to Me—Is The Basis of The Way of Adidam. If I am heart-recognized, you "Know" (or Tacitly Apprehend) My Divine Avataric Person and State—and, Thus and Thereby, you "Know" (or Tacitly Apprehend) The Divine Avataric Self-Revelation.

If I am heart-recognized, all "God"-ideas are transcended—in The Unmediated Self-Revelation of The Divine Reality (and Self-Condition) Itself. And That Unmediated Self-Revelation makes possible a Unique Way.

The only-by-Me Revealed and Given Way of Adidam is Prior to the exercises of egoity and self-contraction, Prior to all forms of seeking.

The only-by-Me Revealed and Given Way of Adidam Is truly The Way of Most Perfect Real-God-Realization, or The Realization of The Self-Condition and Self-Domain That <u>Is</u> The Inherently egoless, Perfectly Indivisible, and Perfectly Acausal Divine.

Therefore, The Way of Adidam is not about any kind of egoic exercise. Rather, The Way of Adidam is, from the beginning, about the inherent transcending of ego in The Divine Self-Condition Itself. Such is the nature of true heart-recognition of Me and true heart-Communion with Me. Such is The Uniqueness of The Way I have Revealed and Given.

The Way of Adidam Is The Unique Revelation of The Divine <u>Itself</u>. And The Way of Adidam Is The Unique Divine Avataric Way of practice.

If I am heart-recognized, This is What you (Thus and Thereby) "Know".

III.

The attempt to account for the apparently arising conditional world by postulating a "First Cause" is fundamental to both Western and Eastern philosophy since the ancient days. It is the perspective of "point of view" (or egoity) that makes such ideas—and that "point-of-view" perspective is an ancient fault.

"God"-<u>ideas</u> come from ego—and "God"-ideas not only reflect the ego itself, but, altogether, "God"-ideas, being mere ideas, reinforce and console the state of egoity, and, in fact, subordinate The Real Divine to the ego and the ego's search and purpose. The purpose of "God"-ideas is to account for the "objective world" and the "separate self"— by presuming the "objective world" and the "separate self" as the <u>first</u> (and even irreducibly existing) matters of philosophical importance. However, in The Real Process of Real-God-Realization, the first matter of philosophical importance is the <u>prior</u> transcending of the <u>illusions</u> (or the non-ultimacy) of "objective world" and "separate self".

In the usual mode of philosophical or theological thinking, a "First Cause", or a "Prime Mover", or a "Creator-God" is hypothesized, to "explain" the appearance of "objective world" and "separate self", which are presumed to be the irreducible first matters of philosophical importance. Such is ego-based philosophy. And such ego-based philosophy is the entire basis of the "great tradition" of the "great path of return"—or the global manifestation of the (always priorly ego-based, and, thus, necessarily, psycho-physically-based and conditionality-bound) first six stages of life. The philosophy of the first six stages of life always presumes "objective world" and "separate self" (or "point of view" and ego-"I") <u>first</u>.

The Way of Adidam is about transcending the illusory (or self-"objectified") "subjectivity" of "ego" and the illusory (or egoically "objectified") "objectivity" of "world" first. That being the case, The Self-Nature of Reality is The First Evidence to be Realized, not something to be Realized later.

The world is not "Caused". Rather, the world is acausally evident. Any philosophy that is concerned with "Cause" is about the exercise of "point of view" (or egoity).

The tacit understanding of The Divine <u>As</u> The Intrinsic Self-Condition of Reality Itself—and, Thus, <u>As</u> The Self-Nature, or Reality-Nature, That <u>Is</u> Inherently egoless, Indivisible, and Acausal—tacitly (and Inherently, or Priorly, and Perfectly) transcends not merely the characteristics of Western and Eastern philosophy, but also the fundamental basis and the total enterprise of the entire "great tradition", even in its most ancient historically evident traditions and modes of thinking, seeking, and practicing.

If you take up the position of "ego", then you have a "problem", and you have an apparently "objective" reality for which to account. Merely to take up the ego-position generates an entire system of modes of thinking and seeking. That system, in its entirety, <u>is</u> the first six stages of life, which characterize the "great tradition" (or "great path of return").

That first-six-stages-of-life system is not The Way of Adidam. The Way of Adidam is characterized by a unique (and tacit) philosophical understanding—an understanding that is unique in relation to all the modes of philosophizing that underlie the "great tradition" (or "great path of return"), and also unique in relation to all the modes of academic philosophizing.

If you presume the world and the separate-self-principle first, then you have already commanded (or determined) the fundamental characteristics of your philosophy. In that case, you have already based everything on "point of view"—on what appears to be the case when "point of view" is priorly presumed to be "the way things are".

To illustrate The Intrinsic (egoless and Indivisible and Acausal) Self-Condition of Reality Itself, I have often used the metaphor of a room, in which any number of people may be sitting. Each person in the "room" would describe the "room" (or, by extension, the world, or the universe) in a certain manner, based on his or her particular position within the "room" (or his or her "location" in space and time). Similarly, if any person in the "room" held a camera and took a photograph of the "room", the "room" would appear ("objectively") as it does from his or her particular position. The photograph would be "true" as a matter of concrete observation—in basic terms of how the "room" looks from that particular position. Thus, the any snapshot is "real" from the perspective of its particular "point of view". However, no such snapshot characterizes the "room" <u>itself</u>— <u>As</u> it <u>Is</u>, or <u>As Is</u>, and, Thus, <u>As</u> Reality Itself.

What about all the other possible "points of view", all the other possible photographs? If everybody in the "room" took a snapshot of the "room" from where they were sitting, each photograph would present a different appearance (or description) of the "room". How many photographs would be necessary and sufficient to <u>totally</u> account for the "room"—or the world, or the universe?

Can the "room" (or the world, or the universe) <u>itself</u>—<u>As</u> it <u>Is</u>, and as a <u>totality</u> (in the totality of <u>all</u> space-time)—be accounted for, or even "known", from <u>any</u> "point of view", or from even the totality of <u>all</u> "points of view", or from (necessarily, space-time-"located") "point of view" at all? Therefore, is it even possible, from the human psycho-physical perspective, to Really and Perfectly "Know" the very "room" (or the world, or the universe) in which you are even now "located"? Indeed, is it not true that, no matter what arises, you <u>do</u> <u>not</u> (and <u>cannot</u>) "Know" what even a single thing (or any kind of interior or exterior "object") <u>Is</u>?

Remarkably, the actual "room" itself—or the world itself, or the universe as a totality, or even any "object", or even the ego-"I" itself—is <u>never</u> "known" (<u>As</u> it <u>Is</u>). The only and constant event is the "subjective" illusion—or the wandering "point of view" that "knows" the "objective" (or egoically "objectified") changes of necessarily limited and finite "happenings" (or conditionally arising changes of ego-based appearance). That always separate "point of view" (and its presumptions, perceptions, and problems) is the perennial basis for all traditional (or first-six-stages-of-life) philosophy—and, thus, for all traditional and conventional mere (and, necessarily, not-Perfect) ideas about "self", the "world", the "universe", "God", "Truth", and "Reality".

In any moment, the "room" (or any particular space-time-"location") <u>itself</u>—and Reality <u>Itself</u>—already (apparently) exists, or else no position within the "room" (or within The Context of Reality Itself) could describe "it". Nevertheless, the "room" itself is <u>not</u> as it seems to be from any particular "point of view". The "room" itself is <u>not</u> even as it would seem to be from the collectively self-accumulated perspective of all possible "points of view" in time and space. Indeed, the (entirely "point-of-view"-based) presumption that the "room" (or the world, or the universe, or the space-time context of conditionally arising apparent experience) is (Really, and irreducibly) "objectively" existing is the very basis (and the inherently untenable premise) of all conventional (and, necessarily, false, and, ultimately, failed) philosophy.

No accumulation of "points of view" can ever comprehend the "room" As it Is—not merely in either physical or metaphysical terms, but simply As it Is. What is The Condition within Which the "room" is apparent? That Condition is not something reducible to any particular "point of view" or even to an infinite number of "points of view". That Condition Is simply As Is—Always Already (or Inherently) Prior to "point of view" (or space-time-"location") itself, and, therefore, Prior to all "objective" appearances, measurements, and experiences.

Even though any particular "room" could, in principle, be perceived from an infinite number of particular "points of view", the "room" itself is (As it Is) inherently Prior to all "points of view". No "point-of-view"-description can account for the "room" itself.

The "room", or the world, or the universe, or the space-time continuum—or even anyone or anything at all—is not an "object". This is a remarkable fact—but it is Self-Evidently True.

Therefore, to account for Reality Itself—or even for the world itself, or the total universe, or any apparent "object", or for The Real Condition of "self"—"point of view" must not be assumed a priori, or as a first principle—nor, in Reality, is the "objective world" (as it may be said to exist from any "point of view") a first principle (or an irreducible characteristic of Reality Itself). Indeed, the presumption of "objective world" and the presumption of "objective separate-self-principle" must (and always as the first principle) be Perfectly <u>transcended</u>—or else it is self-evidently <u>impossible</u> for right and true (and Inherently Perfect, and True-To-Reality-Itself) philosophy to be made or done.

Therefore, Perfect Philosophy (Which is The Philosophy associated with The Way of Adidam) is, necessarily, Prior to "point of view", Prior to the presumption of "separate self" and "objective world".

"Point of view" defines "separate self" and "objective world". Therefore, "point of view" defines whatever is sought—including The Divine. From the position of "point of view", The Divine is described as "Cause" (or "Creator")—but, Prior to "point of view", Prior to "separate self" and "objective world", The Divine Is simply (or Tacitly and Intrinsically) Self-Evident, and of an Inherently egoless, Perfectly Indivisible, and Perfectly Acausal Nature. Such is The Perfect Philosophy That Is The Basis of The Way of Adidam. Therefore, on the basis of That Perfect Philosophy (and as The Necessary, Tacit, and Always Prior Exercise of The Inherent First Principle of That Perfect Philosophy), the "point-of-view"-presumptions of "separate self" and of "objective world" are, from the very beginning of The Way of Adidam, transcended "at the root". Therefore, even though the process of The Way of Adidam can, to some extent, be described in philosophical terms, the process itself is not a philosophical (or mental) exercise of analysis, calculation, and problem-solving. The process of The Way of Adidam is about total psycho-physical turning to Me <u>on sight</u>, heart-moved by The Self-Evident Reality That <u>Is</u> "Perfectly Known" (or Tacitly Self-Apprehended) by simply heart-recognizing Me.

The true devotional recognition-response to Me is Inherently (and Inherently Perfectly) egoless and Indivisible and Acausal. Heart-recognition of Me is recognition of The

Inherently egoless, Perfectly Indivisible, and Perfectly Acausal Nature of Reality Itself, Which is Realized (in heart-Communion with Me) to Be The One and Indivisible Self-Existing, Self-Radiant, and Self-Evidently Divine Conscious Light Itself. In That Divinely Avatarically Self-Revealed Reality-State, everything apparently arising is a transparent (or merely apparent), and non-necessary, and inherently egoless (or inherently non-binding) modification of The Divine Self-Condition Itself (or The Transcendental and Spiritual Divine Conscious Light Itself).

IV.

In Reality, there is no "separate self"—as such.

There Is Only The One and Indivisible Divine Conscious Light.

Whatever apparent modification there may seem to be—in the form of a body or a brain or an event in time and space—There Is Only The Inherently egoless, and One, and Perfectly Indivisible, and Perfectly Acausal, and Self-Evidently Divine Reality (or Self-Condition).

I can Spontaneously Speak This, because This Is My Intrinsically Self-Evident and Perfectly Non-conditional State of Self-Realization—Of That, In That, and As That.

I Am That.

When I am heart-recognized, the process that occurs goes Beyond "point of view", and Beyond self-contraction. That process is about the responsive turning to Me, and heart-Communion with Me, and (in due course) participation in My Spiritual Self-Transmission, to the point (Ultimately) of Most Perfect Realization—transcending the root of egoity itself, on the basis of "radical" (or always already "at-the-root") devotion to Me.

That process is demonstrated as the constant devotional turning of the principal faculties (of body, emotion, mind, and breath) to Me, and as the (thereby motivated) embrace of right self-discipline (or right life) in accordance with My Instruction (which embrace is true renunciation), and as "Perfect Knowledge" (or The Intrinsic "Knowledge", or Tacit Self-Apprehension) of The by-Me-and-As-Me Divinely Avatarically Self-Transmitted and Self-Revealed Consciousness-Energy (or egoless Indivisible Acausal Conscious Light) That Is The Self-Evident Self-Characteristic of The Divine Self-Condition Itself.

Realization of Me Is The seventh stage Realization—The Most Perfect Realization of The Inherently egoless and Perfectly Indivisible Conscious Light That Is The Divine Person and Self-Condition and Self-Domain (or Reality Itself).

That Realization is of a Transcendental (and egoless), and Spiritual (and Indivisible), and Divine (and Self-Existing, and Self-Radiant, and Perfectly Acausal) Nature.

V.

Where there is egolessness, there is a right comprehension of the world, the body, and all events—but that right comprehension is not merely a mental phenomenon.

The mind can become a kind of "reflection" of The Inherently egoless State of Divine Self-Realization, but the mind is not, itself, The Source of Realization.

There is no "inner permanent entity" in the human individual.

There Is Only The Self-Existing, Self-Radiant, Inherently egoless, and Self-Evidently Divine Conscious Light.

The Divine Conscious Light is not born—and The Divine Conscious Light does not come to an end in death.

Conditional processes have a kind of continuation, but they have no ultimacy.

Conditional processes arise during (and previous to) the physical lifetime of an individual, and they also continue after the physical lifetime.

Nevertheless, the factuality of such continuation does not mean that there is a permanent internal principle in the human individual.

In Truth, and in Reality, There Is <u>Only</u> The Self-Existing and Self-Radiant Divine Self-Condition Itself.

Everything conditional is a conditionally apparent "play" upon That.

There is no separate "interior absolute", no permanent entity, or "soul", "inside" the human being.

There Is <u>Only</u> The egoless, Indivisible, and Acausally Self-Existing and Self-Radiant Divine Self-Condition.

The apparent human being Inheres, Indivisibly, In That and <u>As</u> That.

The Divine Self-Condition does not merely continue.

The Divine Self-Condition (or egoless Indivisible and Acausal Consciousness-Energy, or Conscious Light) Is Always Already The Case, and (Therefore) "It" cannot be destroyed.

In the workings of the conditional universe, energy neither comes into being nor disappears—rather, energy is always conserved, or perpetually transformed.

So, also, in the case of human beings, That Which Is The Fundamental Identity of any human individual is not born and does not die.

That Which Is The Fundamental Identity (or Intrinsic Self-Condition) does not come into existence, and "It" does not disappear.

Thus, Consciousness-Energy is not simply a characteristic of a mortal human lifetime.

Rather, Consciousness-Energy Is The Fundamental Characteristic (or Always Prior Self-Condition) of all arising.

Consciousness-Energy is not merely a combination of awareness and mind and body.

Consciousness-Energy (and, As Such, Consciousness Itself) Is a Fundamental Characteristic of Reality Itself (or The One and Indivisible and Acausal and Inherently egoless Divine Conscious Light Itself).

The non-human beings—and even so-called "inanimate things"—Are Consciousness-Energy (or The Divine Conscious Light Itself), just as (and as much as) any and every human being.

Everything is an apparent (and never separate, or independent, or irreducibly absolute) modification of The One and Indivisible Divine Conscious Light.

Therefore (and As egoless Conscious Light Itself), no "thing" can be destroyed—and no "one" can be destroyed.

Only the apparent "play" of conditions (seen from "point of view") undergoes a process of apparent modifications and changes.

Reality Itself is never (Within and As "Its" Own Self-Context of Self-Apprehension) modified or changed—but "It" is only conditionally (or merely apparently, or seemingly "objectively", or merely from the perspective, or "location", of "point of view") modified and changed.

The human being can Realize Perfect Coincidence with The birthless and deathless Divine Conscious Light That Is Reality Itself.

The Divine Self-Condition of Conscious Light can be Realized Most Perfectly.

107

That Most Perfect Realization Is Inherently egoless and Non-conditional.

Nevertheless, That Realization Is Perfectly Coincident with the appearance of conditions.

That Realization does not involve or require—or even allow—the slightest degree of dissociation from conditions.

Rather, That Realization, Ultimately, Outshines all conditions—in Divine Translation.[16]

VI.

The only-by-Me Revealed and Given Way of Adidam has nothing to do with egoity.

The only-by-Me Revealed and Given Way of Adidam has nothing to do with seeking.

The only-by-Me Revealed and Given Way of Adidam has nothing to do with problem-solving.

The only-by-Me Revealed and Given Way of Adidam Is The Divine "Radical" Way—Transcending all limitations "at the root", from the beginning.

The only-by-Me Revealed and Given Way of Adidam Is The seventh stage Way.

As Such, The Way of Adidam is not, in any sense, associated with the ego-principle (or "separate self"), or with the overcoming of the ego-principle (by any exercise or means or "point of view" or mode of thinking).

My Divine Avataric Teaching-Revelation Is a Spontaneous Utterance of The egoless Indivisible and Acausal Self-Evidence of Self-Evident Reality Itself.

Thus, The Way of Adidam is Uttered Beyond and Prior to "point of view".

The words I Use are in the mode of human language—which I am Constantly Transforming, in order to Make My Divine Avataric Teaching-Revelation Clear to every one.

Nevertheless, My Divine Avataric Teaching-Revelation is not based on the "point-of-view"-presumption from which the conventions of human language are otherwise generated.

My Divine Avataric Transcendental Spiritual Self-Transmission Is Beyond words.

All words require (in some mode or other) an accommodation to the egoic basis of language.

Therefore, My Divine Avataric Transcendental Spiritual Self-Transmission Is, Essentially, Wordless, or Silent, or Tacit.

The Intrinsic Self-Realization of The Divine Conscious Light Is The Basis for all Right and Intrinsically Divine Utterance.

The Way of Adidam has Been—and, altogether, <u>Is</u>—Self-Revealed, by Me, precisely on That Basis.

The Way of Adidam Is The Way of Conscious Light, Divinely Avatarically Self-Revealed By and <u>As</u> Conscious Light Itself.

The only-by-Me Revealed and Given Way of Adidam Is The Divine and Inherently Perfect Way That Is Divinely Avatarically Self-Revealed By and <u>As</u> Reality Itself. ∎

NOTES TO THE TEXT OF
THE ANCIENT WALK-ABOUT WAY

Introduction

1. For a simple, visual presentation of this evidence, see
www.nationalgeographic.com/genographic/atlas.html.

2. Although this Great Tradition naturally includes the indigenous
Australian cultures (and all human cultures), Adi Da does not use "Walk-
About" in the specific sense that has been used in reference to the
Australian Aborigines.

3. Advayataraka Upanishad 14–18, verse 5.

4. Please see the glossary, **gross, subtle, causal (dimensions)**.

The Super-Physics of Divine Enlightenment

5. Avatar Adi Da is referring here to the unique "seventh stage" nature of
His Description of Divine Self-Realization. Please see glossary, **stages
of life**.

6. Avatar Adi Da uses the terms "childish" and "adolescent" with precise
meanings in His Wisdom-Teaching. He points out that human beings are
always tending to animate one of two fundamental life-strategies—the
childish strategy (to be dependent, weak, seeking to be consoled by parent-
figures and a parent-"God") and the adolescent strategy (to be independent—or, otherwise, torn between independence and dependence—
rebellious, unfeeling, self-absorbed, and doubting or resisting the idea of
God or any power greater than oneself). Until these two strategies are
understood and transcended, they not only diminish love in ordinary
human relations, but they also limit religious and Spiritual growth.

7. Avatar Adi Da Samraj has Revealed that just as there is a physical anatomy,
there is an actual "esoteric anatomy", or hierarchical structural anatomy,
that is present in every human being. As He Says in His Essay "Growing
Beyond the Brain-Based Myth of Materialism", from *The Basket Of
Tolerance*, it is because of this structure that the "experiential and developmental process of Growth and Realization demonstrates itself in accordance with what I have Revealed and Demonstrated to be the seven
stages of life".
   Avatar Adi Da's extended Instruction relative to the hierarchical structural anatomy of the human being is Given in *The Seven Stages Of Life* and
Santosha Adidam.

8. For Avatar Adi Da's description of the full process of Divine Enlightenment, see *The Dawn Horse Testament Of The Ruchira Avatar* or *The Seven Stages Of Life*.

I Am Your Unique Advantage

9. For a description of the developmental stages of practice in the Way of Adidam, see *The Dawn Horse Testament Of The Ruchira Avatar*.

The Supreme Secret of Spiritual Life

10. "Perfect Contemplation" is a technical term Avatar Adi Da uses to describe formal occasions of Communion with Him when the practitioner has been established in the "Perfect Practice" of Adidam (see glossary, **"Perfect Practice"**). "Perfect Contemplation" is no longer any kind of exercise of the faculties of the body-mind (as is "meditation"), but rather is established as effortless "Contemplation" of Avatar Adi Da as Consciousness Itself, Prior to body and mind.

11. To be "intoxicated" with Avatar Adi Da's Divine Love-Bliss is to be drawn beyond the usual egoic self and egoic mind into a state of ecstatic devotional Communion (and Identification) with Him. This term is enclosed in quotation marks in order to distinguish it from the common meaning of "intoxication" (such as with alcohol).

The Ancient Walk-About Way

12. Avatar Adi Da uses the term "outer temple" in a manner comparable to the term "exoteric", as opposed to esoteric (or "inner temple"). Thus, the "outer temple" of Adidam is the preparatory "novice" period of student-beginner practice and establishing of the life-disciplines.

13. Avatar Adi Da coined the term "klik-klak" as a name for conditional reality. This name indicates (even by means of the sound of the two syllables) that conditional reality is a heartless perpetual-motion machine of incessant change, producing endlessly varied patterns that are (at root) binary in nature (as, for example, "yes-no", "on-off", or "black-white").

14. *Fifty Verses of Guru Devotion* is a Buddhist text attributed to Asvaghosa (first century CE), detailing the sacred laws of the relationship between the Guru (or Spiritual Master) and the devotee.

True Devotion <u>Is</u> "Perfect Knowledge" Demonstrated By Renunciation

15. There are four modes of formal association with Avatar Adi Da Samraj—known as the four "congregations" of His devotees. Each congregation has its own particular form of relationship to Avatar Adi Da, and its own degree of participation in the formal practice of the Way of Adidam. Adi Da has created the four congregations in order to make it possible for anyone to participate in the formal relationship to Him. The total practice of the Way of Adidam is engaged only by those in the first and second congregations, which Avatar Adi Da calls the congregations of His "formally practicing devotees" (or "formally acknowledged devotees"). The first congregation is comprised of Avatar Adi Da's renunciate devotees, who are members of the Ruchira Sannyasin Order of Adidam Ruchiradam or the Lay Renunciate Order of Adidam Ruchiradam. The second congregation is the general (or lay) gathering of His devotees. Members of the first and second congregations are vowed to engage the full range of devotional and supportive disciplines (meditation, sacramental worship, guided study, exercise, diet, emotional-sexual discipline, cooperative culture, and so on) Given by Avatar Adi Da Samraj.

Perfect Adidam

16. Avatar Adi Da has Revealed that the Awakening to the seventh stage of life is not an "endpoint" but is (rather) the beginning of the final Spiritual process. One of the unique aspects of Avatar Adi Da's Revelation is His precise description of the seventh stage process as consisting of four phases: Divine Transfiguration, Divine Transformation, Divine Indifference, and Divine Translation. "Outshine" and its variants refer to the process of Divine Translation, the final Demonstration of this four-phase process. In the Great Event of Outshining (or Divine Translation), body, mind, and world are no longer noticed—not because one has withdrawn or dissociated from conditionally manifested phenomena, but because the Self-Abiding Divine Self-Recognition of all arising phenomena as modifications of the Divine Self-Condition has become so intense that the "Bright" Divine Conscious Light now Outshines all such phenomena.

GLOSSARY

Adidam—In January 1996, when Avatar Adi Da Samraj first Gave the name "Adidam" to the Way He has Revealed, He pointed out that the final "m" adds a mantric force, evoking the effect of the primal Sanskrit syllable "Om". (For Avatar Adi Da's Revelation of the most profound esoteric significance of "Om" as the Divine Sound of His own Very Being, see *The Dawn Horse Testament*.) Simultaneously, the final "m" suggests the English word "Am" (expressing "I Am"), such that the name "Adidam" also evokes Avatar Adi Da's Primal Self-Confession, "I Am Adi Da", or, more simply, "I Am Da".

Alpha and Omega—Avatar Adi Da calls the characteristic traditional Eastern strategy the "Alpha" strategy. Alpha cultures pursue an undisturbed peace, in which the conditional world is excluded as much as possible from attention (and thereby ceases to be a disturbance). Although the cultures that were originally founded on the Alpha approach to life and Truth are fast disappearing, the Alpha strategy remains the conventional archetype of Spiritual life, even in the Omega culture. In contrast to the Omega preference, the Alpha preference is to limit and control (and even suppress) attention to the conditional reality, while maximizing attention to the Divine Reality.

Avatar Adi Da uses the term "Omega" to characterize the materialistic culture that today dominates not only the Western world (which has brought the Omega strategy to its fullest development) but even most of the present-day Eastern world, which has now largely adopted the anti-Spiritual viewpoint typical of the West. The Omega strategy is motivated to the attainment of a future-time perfection and fulfillment of the conditional worlds, through the intense application of human invention, political will, and even Divine Influence. Its preference is to limit and suppress attention to the Divine Reality, while maximizing attention to the conditional reality.

Neither the Alpha strategy nor the Omega strategy Realizes Truth absolutely, as each is rooted in the presumption of a "problem" relative to existence. (For Avatar Adi Da's extended discussion of the Alpha and Omega strategies, see *The Truly Human New World-Culture Of Unbroken Real-God-Man*.)

Avataric Incarnation—The Divinely Descended Embodiment of the Divine Person. The reference "Avataric Incarnation" indicates that Avatar Adi Da Samraj fulfills both the traditional expectation of the East, that the True God-Man is an Avatar (or an utterly Divine "Descent" of Real Acausal God in conditionally manifested form), and the traditional expectation of the West, that the True God-Man is an Incarnation (or an utterly human Embodiment of Real Acausal God).

"Bright"—By the word "Bright" (and its variations, such as "Brightness"), Avatar Adi Da refers to the Self-Existing and Self-Radiant Divine Reality that He has Revealed since His Birth. Avatar Adi Da Named His own Self-Evidently Divine Self-Condition "the 'Bright'" in His Infancy, as soon as He acquired the capability of language.

This term is placed in quotation marks to indicate that Avatar Adi Da uses it with the specific meaning described here.

"Bright" Divine Spherical Self-Domain—*See* **Self-Domain, "Bright" Divine Spherical**.

Divine Form, Presence, and State—Avatar Adi Da Samraj has Revealed that He Exists simultaneously in three Divine Avataric Forms—physical (His bodily human Form), Spiritual (His Spiritual Presence), and the Formlessness of Self-Existing and Self-Radiant Consciousness Itself (His Very State). The fundamental practice of heart-Communion with Him includes heart-Communion with all three aspects of His Being—always (from the very beginning of the practice of the Way of Adidam through the seventh stage of life) founded in devotional recognition-response to His Avatarically-Born bodily (human) Divine Form and Person.

ego-"I"—The fundamental activity of self-contraction, or the presumption of separate and separative existence.

The "I" is placed in quotation marks to indicate that it is used by Avatar Adi Da in the "so to speak" sense. He is Communicating (by means of the quotation marks) that, in Reality, there is no such thing as the separate "I", even though it appears to be the case from the "point of view" of ordinary human perception.

"evolutionary"—Avatar Adi Da uses the term "evolution" and its variants to indicate the goal-oriented struggle to fulfill the potential of the human body-mind, or the "great path of return".

These terms are placed in quotation marks to indicate the sense of "so to speak", in relation to the false presumption that Real-God-Realization is based on a necessary evolution by means of the "great path of return" rather than directly living on the basis of present-time relationship with the Divine.

faculties (of the body-mind)—Body, emotion (or feeling), mind (or attention), and breath. These four principal faculties account for the entirety of the human being. The practice of Ruchira Avatara Bhakti Yoga (or heart-Communion with Avatar Adi Da) is, fundamentally, the moment

to moment turning of the four principal faculties to Him. *See also*
turn/turning (to Adi Da Samraj).

Form, Presence, and State—*See* **Divine Form, Presence, and State**.

functional, practical, relational, and cultural disciplines—The most
basic <u>functional</u>, <u>practical</u>, and <u>relational</u> <u>disciplines</u> of the Way of Adidam
are forms of appropriate human action and responsibility in relation to diet,
health, exercise, sexuality, work, service to and support of Avatar Adi Da's
Circumstance and Work, and cooperative association with other practition-
ers of the Way of Adidam. The most basic <u>cultural</u> <u>obligations</u> of the Way of
Adidam include meditation, sacramental worship, study of Avatar Adi Da's
Wisdom-Teaching (and also at least a basic discriminative study of the
Great Tradition of religion and Spirituality that is the Wisdom-inheritance of
humankind), and regular participation in the "form" (or schedule) of daily,
weekly, monthly, and annual devotional activities and retreats.

"great path of return"—Avatar Adi Da characterizes the traditional religious
and Spiritual paths of the first six stages of life as the "great path of return"
because the traditional "points of view" associated with the first six stages of
life regard the "goal" of the Spiritual path to be somewhere "else" than
"here". In other words, it is traditionally presumed that the Spiritual Way is a
matter of following a "great path" by which the aspirant will "return" from
"here" to the "place" that is regarded to be the "goal" (or "home").

   Right practice of the Way of Adidam, on the other hand, is not a matter of seeking to reach any of the "goals" of the first six stages of life, but
is (rather) a matter of practicing (progressively) <u>in</u> <u>the</u> <u>context</u> <u>of</u> the first
six stages of life, while persistently observing, understanding, and tran-
scending all forms of motivated seeking as they arise.

   This term is placed in quotation marks to indicate that Avatar Adi Da
uses it with the specific technical meaning described here.

Great Tradition—The Great Tradition is Avatar Adi Da's term for the
total inheritance of human, cultural, religious, magical, mystical, Spiritual,
and Transcendental paths, philosophies, and testimonies, from all the eras
and cultures of humankind—which inheritance has (in the present era of
worldwide communication) become the common legacy of humankind.
The Way of Adidam is the Divine Way in Which the entire Great Tradition
of humankind is at once culminated and transcended.

gross, subtle, causal (dimensions)—Avatar Adi Da (in agreement with
certain esoteric schools in the Great Tradition) describes conditional existence as having three fundamental dimensions—gross, subtle, and causal.

   "Gross" means "made up of material (or physical) elements". The
gross (or physical) dimension is, therefore, associated with the physical

body. The gross dimension is also associated with experience in the waking state and, as Avatar Adi Da Reveals, with the frontal line of the body-mind and with the left side of the heart (or the gross physical heart).

The subtle dimension, which is senior to and pervades the gross dimension, consists of the etheric (or personal life-energy) functions, the lower mental functions (including the conscious mind, the subconscious mind, and the unconscious mind) and higher mental functions (of discriminative mind, mentally presumed egoity, and will), and is associated with experience in the dreaming state. In the human psycho-physical structure, the subtle dimension is primarily associated with the middle station of the heart (or the heart chakra), the spinal line, the brain core, and the subtle centers of mind in the higher brain.

The causal dimension is senior to both the gross and the subtle dimensions. It is the root of attention, or the root-sense of existence as a separate self. The causal dimension is associated with the right side of the heart, specifically with the sinoatrial node, or "pacemaker" (the psycho-physical source of the heartbeat). Its corresponding state of consciousness is the formless awareness of deep sleep.

"late-time" (or "dark" epoch)—Avatar Adi Da uses the terms "late-time" and "'dark' epoch" to describe the present era—in which doubt of God (and of anything at all beyond mortal existence) is more and more pervading the entire world, and the self-interest of the separate individual is more and more regarded to be the ultimate principle of life.

These terms include quotation marks to indicate that they are used by Avatar Adi Da in the "so to speak" sense. In this case, He is Communicating (by means of the quotation marks) that, in Reality, the "darkness" of this apparent "late-time" is not Reality, or Truth, but only an appearance from the "point of view" of ordinary human perception.

Most Perfect / Most Ultimate—Avatar Adi Da uses the phrase "Most Perfect(ly)" in the sense of "Absolutely Perfect(ly)". Similarly, the phrase "Most Ultimate(ly)" is equivalent to "Absolutely Ultimate(ly)". "Most Perfect(ly)" and "Most Ultimate(ly)" are always references to the seventh (or Divinely Enlightened) stage of life. "Perfect(ly)" and "Ultimate(ly)" (without "Most") refer to the practice and Realization in the context of the "Perfect Practice" of the Way of Adidam (or, when Avatar Adi Da is making reference to the Great Tradition, to practice and Realization in the context of the sixth stage of life).

mummery—The dictionary defines "mummery" as "a ridiculous, hypocritical, or pretentious ceremony or performance". Avatar Adi Da uses this word to describe all the activities of ego-bound beings, or beings who are committed to the false view of separation and separativeness.

Omega—*See* **Alpha and Omega**.

"Perfect Practice"—The "Perfect Practice" is Avatar Adi Da's technical term for the discipline of the most mature stages of practice in the Way of Adidam. The "Perfect Practice" is practice in the Domain of Consciousness Itself (as opposed to practice from the "point of view" of the body or the mind). The "Perfect Practice" unfolds in three phases, the third of which is Divine Enlightenment. This term is placed in quotation marks to indicate that Avatar Adi Da uses it with the specific technical meaning described here.

Perfectly Subjective—Avatar Adi Da uses this phrase to describe the True Divine Source (or "Subject") of the conditionally manifested worlds—as opposed to regarding the Acausal Divine as some sort of objective "Other". Thus, in the phrase "Perfectly Subjective", the word "Subjective" does not have the sense of "relating to the inward experience of an individual", but, rather, it has the sense of "Being Consciousness Itself, the True 'Subject' of all apparent experience".

"point of view"—In Avatar Adi Da's Wisdom-Teaching, "point of view" is placed in quotation marks to indicate that Avatar Adi Da uses this term in the "so to speak" sense. He is Communicating (by means of the quotation marks) that, in Reality, there is no such thing as a "point of view", even though it is presumed to be the case in ordinary human perception. Avatar Adi Da uses this phrase as another way to describe the ego-"I".

preliminary practice of "Perfect Knowledge"—Avatar Adi Da's offering of a practice that tacitly "locates" the "Perfect Knowledge" of His State, for those who are yet identified with the faculties of the conditional body-mind. The Teachings and practice are "preliminary" because they are intended to lead to the true practice of "Perfect Knowledge", which is established in the context of the "Perfect Practice" of Adidam, when all identification with the conditional body and mind are transcended. The preliminary "Perfect Knowledge" practice is to be practiced in perpetual conjunction with the foundation practice of Ruchira Avatara Bhakti Yoga.

puja—The ceremonial worship of Avatar Adi Da, typically conducted by adorning His Murti with flowers and anointing It with elements such as sandalwood oil and sacred ash.

"radical"—Derived from the Latin "radix", meaning "root". Thus, "radical" principally means "irreducible", "fundamental", or "relating to the origin". Thus, Avatar Adi Da defines "radical" as "at-the-root". Because Adi Da Samraj uses "radical" in this literal sense, it appears in quotation marks in His Wisdom-Teaching, in order to distinguish His usage from the common reference to an extreme (often political) view.

Real (Acausal) God—The True (and Perfectly Subjective) Source of all conditions, the True and Spiritual Divine Person—rather than any ego-made (and, thus, false, or limited) presumption about God.

Ruchira Avatara Bhakti Yoga—Ruchira Avatara Bhakti Yoga is the principal Gift, Calling, and Discipline Offered by Avatar Adi Da Samraj to His devotees.

The phrase "Ruchira Avatara Bhakti Yoga" is itself a summary of the Way of Adidam. "Bhakti", in Sanskrit, is "love, adoration, or devotion", while "Yoga" is "Real-God-Realizing discipline, or practice". "Ruchira Avatara Bhakti Yoga" is, thus, "the practice of devotion to the Ruchira Avatar, Adi Da Samraj".

The practice of Ruchira Avatara Bhakti Yoga is the process of turning the four principal faculties (body, emotion, mind, and breath) to Avatar Adi Da (in and <u>as</u> His Avatarically-Born bodily human Divine Form) in every moment and under all circumstances.

self-contraction—The fundamental presumption (and activity) of separation.

Self-Domain, "Bright" Divine Spherical—Avatar Adi Da affirms that there is a Divine Self-Domain that is the Perfectly Subjective Condition of the conditional worlds. It is not "elsewhere", not an objective "place" (like a subtle "heaven" or mythical "paradise"), but It is the Self-Evidently Divine Source-Condition of every conditionally manifested being and thing—and It is not other than Avatar Adi Da Himself. Avatar Adi Da Reveals that His Divine Self-Domain is a Boundless (and Boundlessly "Bright") Sphere. To Realize the seventh stage of life (by the Divine Spiritual Grace of Avatar Adi Da Samraj) is to Awaken to His Divine Self-Domain. See *The Dawn Horse Testament*.

Self-Existing and Self-Radiant—"Self-Existing" and "Self-Radiant" are terms describing the two fundamental (and inherent) aspects of the One Divine Person (or Reality)—Existence (or Being, or Consciousness) Itself, and Radiance (or Energy, or Light) Itself.

Siddha-Guru—"Siddha" is Sanskrit for "a completed, fulfilled, or perfected one", or "one of perfect accomplishment, or power". Avatar Adi Da uses "Siddha-Guru" to mean a Transmission-Master who is a Realizer (to any significant degree) of Real (Acausal) God, Truth, or Reality.

stages of life—Avatar Adi Da Samraj describes the experiences and Realizations of humankind in terms of seven stages of life. This schema is one of Avatar Adi Da's unique Gifts to humanity—His precise "mapping" of the potential developmental course of human experience as it unfolds through the gross, subtle, and causal dimensions of the being. He describes this course in terms of six stages of life—which account for, and correspond to, all possible orientations to religion and culture that have arisen in human history. His own Avataric Revelation—the Realization of the "Bright", Prior to all experience—is the seventh stage of life. Understanding this structure of seven stages illuminates the unique nature of Avatar Adi Da's "Sadhana Years" (and of the Spiritual process in His Company).

The first three (or foundation) stages of life constitute the ordinary course of human adaptation—characterized (respectively) by bodily, emotional, and mental growth. Each of the first three stages of life takes approximately seven years to be established. Every individual who lives to an adult age inevitably adapts (although, generally speaking, only partially) to the first three stages of life. In the general case, this is where the developmental process stops—at the gross level of adaptation. Religions based fundamentally on beliefs and moral codes (without direct experience of the dimensions beyond the material world) belong to this foundation level of human development.

The fourth stage of life is characterized by a deep impulse to Communion with the Divine. It is in the context of the fourth stage of life (when one is no longer wedded to the purposes of the first three stages of life) that the true Spiritual process can begin. In the history of the Great Tradition, those involved in the process of the fourth stage of life have characteristically felt the Divine to be a great "Other", in Whom they aspired to become absorbed, through devotional love and service. However, in the Way of Adidam, the presumption that the Divine is "Other" is transcended from the beginning.

In the Way of Adidam, the process of the first three stages of life is lived on the basis of the devotional heart-impulse that is otherwise characteristic of the fourth stage of life. No matter what the age of the individual who comes to Avatar Adi Da, there will generally be signs of failed adaptation to the first three stages of life. But the practice is not a matter of attempting to overcome such failed adaptation through one's own (inevitably egoic) effort or struggle. Rather, the practice is to turn the faculties of the body-mind to Avatar Adi Da in devotional surrender. In that manner, the virtue of the fourth stage of life—the devotional heart-impulse to Commune with the Divine—is specifically animated from the beginning, in living response to Avatar Adi Da. Thus, whatever must be done to righten the first three stages of life occurs in the devotional context of heart-Communion with Him.

Avatar Adi Da has Revealed that the true Spiritual process, beginning in the fully-established (or "basic") context of the fourth stage of life, involves two great dimensions—which He calls the "vertical" and the "horizontal".

The descending aspect of the vertical process characterizes the fourth stage of life, while the ascending aspect characterizes the fifth stage of life. As it has been known in the history of the Great Tradition, the fifth-stage process is the ascent toward absorption into the Divine Matrix of Light Infinitely Above, thereby (ultimately) Realizing the Divine as Light (or Energy) Itself. (Although this Realization is a true "taste" of the Divine Self-Condition, It is achieved by means of the conditional effort of ascent—and, therefore, the Realization Itself is also conditional, or non-permanent.) The fifth stage of life is the ultimate process associated with the subtle dimension of existence.

The horizontal process characterizes the sixth stage of life. As it has been known in the history of the Great Tradition, the sixth stage process is the exclusion of all awareness of the "outside" world (in both its gross and subtle dimensions), by "secluding" oneself within the heart—in order to rest in the Divine Self, Realized (ultimately) as Consciousness Itself. (Like the ultimate Realization associated with the fifth stage of life, the sixth stage Realization is also a true "taste" of the Divine Self-Condition. However, It is also achieved by conditional means—the conditional effort of exclusion—and, therefore, the Realization Itself is also conditional, or non-permanent.) The sixth stage of life is the process associated with the causal dimension of existence.

As Avatar Adi Da has pointed out, even though the fifth stage and sixth stage processes are, in fact, stages in the single process that culminates in Most Perfect Divine Enlightenment (or the seventh stage Realization uniquely Given by Him), the typical traditional view has been that the two processes are alternative approaches to Spiritual Realization. Indeed, these approaches (of either going "Up" or going "Deep") have usually been regarded to be incompatible with each other.

In the Way of Adidam, the "Perfect Practice" encompasses both the vertical process (otherwise characteristically associated with the fifth stage of life) and the horizontal process (otherwise characteristically associated with the sixth stage of life). Thus, in the Way of Adidam, there is no "preference" exercised in favor of either the "Upward" process or the "Inward" process—either the Realization of the Divine as Light Itself or the Realization of the Divine as Consciousness Itself. In the Way of Adidam, both the ultimate "Upward" Realization and the ultimate "Inward" Realization are Freely Given by Avatar Adi Da to the rightly pre-pared and rightly practicing devotee. No effort—either of ascent or of exclusion—is required. And, in fact, all such effort must be inspected, understood, and transcended.

This unique and unprecedented orientation to the developmental processes of the fifth and the sixth stages of life is made possible by the full reception of Avatar Adi Da's Gift of Divine Spiritual Transmission. When the devotee (in the context of the fourth stage of life in the Way of Adidam) is fully open to Avatar Adi Da's Divine Spiritual Transmission, His Divine Spiritual Descent takes over the body-mind, showing specific Yogic signs. In this Yogic Process of Spiritual Descent, there is a profound turnabout in one's awareness of Him. While still always turning to Him devotionally in His bodily (human) Divine Form, one begins to recognize Him, Spiritually, as Consciousness Itself—the Root-Position of existence, Prior to all that is arising in body, mind, and world. This recognition is Spiritually established—and it is the basis for making the transition to the "Perfect Practice" of the Way of Adidam. It is a profound shift, away from identification with the body-mind. From this point on, Avatar Adi Da's Revelation of His own Condition of Consciousness Itself becomes the Position in which one Stands, and from That Position the phenomena associated with both the fifth stage of life and the sixth stage of life will arise. In the "Perfect Practice", one is no longer practicing from the "point of view" of the body-mind and its faculties. Now, devotional turning to Him (or Ruchira Avatara Bhakti Yoga) takes the form of simply "choosing" to Stand in His Position (rather than the ego-position)—inspecting and feeling beyond the root-tendency to contract and create the self-identity called "I".

The seventh stage of life, or the Realization of Avatar Adi Da's own "Bright" Divine Condition, transcends the entire course of human potential. In the seventh stage of life, the impulse to Realize the Divine (as Light) by going "Up" and the impulse to Realize the Divine (as Consciousness) by going "Deep" are (by Avatar Adi Da's Divine Spiritual Grace) <u>simultaneously</u> fulfilled. In that fulfillment, Avatar Adi Da Samraj <u>Himself</u> is most perfectly Realized. He is Realized as the "Bright", the Single Divine Unity of Consciousness and Energy—or Conscious Light Itself. This Most Perfect Realization, or Divine Enlightenment—unique to Avatar Adi Da's Divine Avataric Revelation—wipes away every trace of dissociation from the body-mind and the world. There is no impulse to seek or to avoid any experience. Rather, everything that arises is Divinely Self-Recognized to be merely a modification of the Conscious Light of Reality Itself.

The seventh stage Realization is absolutely Unconditional. It does not depend on any form of effort by the individual. Rather, It is a Divine Gift, Given by Avatar Adi Da to the devotee who has utterly surrendered all egoity to Him. Therefore, the seventh stage Realization is permanent.

Altogether, the Way of Adidam is not about dwelling in (or seeking to either attain or avoid) any of the potential experiences of the first six stages of life. The Way of Adidam is about transcending the entire structure of the human being and of the conditional reality—gross, subtle, and causal. Therefore, the Way of Adidam transcends both the urge to "have" experiences and the urge to "exclude" experience. The Way of Adidam is based, from the beginning, on Avatar Adi Da's "Bright" State, Which is Realized progressively (and, ultimately, most perfectly), by means of His Divine Spiritual Descent in the body-mind of His devotee.

Transcendental Spiritual / Transcendental Spirituality—A reference to the unique "Radical" Way Given and Revealed by Avatar Adi Da

Samraj. The two terms point to the two fundamental (and inherent) aspects of the One Divine Person (or Reality): "Transcendental" refers to Existence (or Being, or Consciousness) Itself and "Spiritual" refers to Energy, or Light) Itself. Therefore, "Transcendental Spiritual" indicates that the practice in Adidam takes place, progresses, and (ultimately) culminates in Most Perfect Divine Self-Realization, in the context of Avatar Adi Da's Self-Revelation of the Inherent Coincidence of the two Ultimate and Co-equal Dimensions of Reality Itself, or the One and Only and Inherently Indivisible Conscious Light Itself (Self-Existing Transcendental Consciousness and Self-Radiant Spirit-Energy).

turn/turning (to Adi Da Samraj)—"Turning" the faculties to Adi Da Samraj is a simple description of the primary practice of the Way of Adidam, which is also called "Ruchira Avatara Bhakti Yoga". *See also* **Ruchira Avatara Bhakti Yoga**.

Way of Adidam—*See* **Adidam**.

The Divine Avataric Great Sage,
ADI DA SAMRAJ

Become a Formal Devotee of Avatar Adi Da Samraj

I n the depth of every human being, there is a profound need for answers to the fundamental questions of existence. Is there a God? What is beyond this life? Why is there suffering? What is Truth? What is Reality?

In this book, you have been introduced to the Wisdom-Revelation of Avatar Adi Da, whose Teachings truly and completely address all of these fundamental questions. How can Avatar Adi Da resolve these fundamental questions? Because He speaks, not from the "point of view" of the human dilemma, but directly from the unique Freedom of His Divine State. Adi Da's Birth in 1939 was an intentional embrace of the human situation, for the sake of Revealing the Way of Divine Liberation to all and Offering the Spiritual Blessing that carries beings to that true Freedom. He is thus the fulfillment of the ancient intuitions of the "Avatar"—the One Who Appears in human Form, as a direct manifestation of the Unmanifest Reality.

Through a 28-year process of Teaching-Work (beginning in 1972), Avatar Adi Da established the Way of Adidam—the Way of the devotional and Spiritual relationship to Him. In those years of Teaching, He spoke for many hours with groups of His devotees—always looking for them, as representatives of humanity, to ask all of their questions about God, Truth, Reality, and human life. In response, He Gave the ecstatic Way of heart-Communion with Him, and all the details of how that process unfolds. Thus, He created a new tradition, based on His direct Revelation (as Avatar) of the Divine Reality.

Avatar Adi Da Samraj does not offer you a set of beliefs, or even a set of Spiritual techniques. He simply Offers you His Revelation of Truth as a Free Gift. If you are moved to take up His Way, He invites you to enter into an extraordinarily deep and transformative devotional and Spiritual relationship to Him. On the following pages, we present a number of ways you can choose to deepen your response to Adi Da Samraj and consider becoming His formal devotee.

To find Avatar Adi Da Samraj is to find the Very Heart of Reality—tangibly felt in your own heart as the Deepest Truth of Existence. This is the great mystery that you are invited to discover. ∎

A*didam is not a conventional religion.
Adidam is not a conventional way of life.
Adidam is about the transcending of the ego-"I".
Adidam is about the Freedom of Divine Self-Realization.*

*Adidam is not based on mythology or belief.
Adidam is a "reality practice".
Adidam is a "reality consideration", in which the various modes of egoity are progressively transcended.*

*Adidam is a universally applicable Way of life.
Adidam is for those who will choose It, and whose hearts and intelligence fully respond to Me and My Offering.
Adidam is a Great Revelation, and It is to be freely and openly communicated to all.*

AVATAR ADI DA SAMRAJ

For what you can do next to respond to Avatar Adi Da's Offering, or to simply find out more about Him and the Way of Adidam, please use the information given in the following pages.

Contact an Adidam center near you for courses and events
(p. 128)

Visit our website: www.adidam.org
(p. 129)

For young people: Join the Adidam Youth Fellowship
(p. 130)

Support Avatar Adi Da's Work and the Way of Adidam
(p. 130)

Order other books and recordings by and about Avatar Adi Da Samraj
(pp. 131–37)

Contact an Adidam center near you

■ To find out about becoming a formal devotee of Avatar Adi Da, and for information about upcoming courses, events, and seminars in your area:

AMERICAS
12040 North Seigler Road
Middletown, CA 95461 USA
1-707-928-4936

PACIFIC-ASIA
12 Seibel Road
Henderson
Auckland 1008
New Zealand
64-9-838-9114

AUSTRALIA
P.O. Box 244
Kew 3101
Victoria
**1800 ADIDAM
(1800-234-326)**

EUROPE-AFRICA
Annendaalderweg 10
6105 AT Maria Hoop
The Netherlands
31 (0)20 468 1442

THE UNITED KINGDOM
uk@adidam.org
0845-330-1008

INDIA
F-168 Shree Love-Ananda Marg
Rampath, Shyam Nagar Extn.
Jaipur–302 019, India
91 (141) 2293080

EMAIL:
correspondence@adidam.org

■ For more contact information about local Adidam groups, please see **www.adidam.org/centers**

Visit our website: www.adidam.org

■ **SEE AUDIO-VISUAL PRESENTATIONS** on the Divine Life and Spiritual Revelation of Avatar Adi Da Samraj

■ **LISTEN TO DISCOURSES** Given by Avatar Adi Da Samraj to His practicing devotees—
  ■ Transcending egoic notions of God
  ■ Why Reality cannot be grasped by the mind
  ■ How the devotional relationship to Avatar Adi Da moves you beyond ego-bondage
  ■ The supreme process of Spiritual Transmission

■ **READ QUOTATIONS** from the "Source-Texts" of Avatar Adi Da Samraj—
  ■ Real God as the only Reality
  ■ The ancient practice of Guru-devotion
  ■ The two opposing life-strategies characteristic of the West and the East—and the way beyond both
  ■ The Prior Unity at the root of all that exists
  ■ The limits of scientific materialism
  ■ The true religion beyond all seeking
  ■ The esoteric structure of the human being
  ■ The real process of death and reincarnation
  ■ The nature of Divine Enlightenment

■ **SUBSCRIBE** to the online *Adidam Revelation* magazine

For young people:
Join the Adidam Youth Fellowship

■ Young people under 21 can participate in the "Adidam Youth Fellowship"—either as a "friend" or practicing member. Adidam Youth Fellowship members participate in study programs, retreats, celebrations, and other events with other young people responding to Avatar Adi Da. To learn more about the Youth Fellowship, call or write:

Vision of Mulund Institute (VMI)
10336 Loch Lomond Road, PMB 146
Middletown, CA 95461
phone: (707) 928-6932
email: vmi@adidam.org
www.visionofmulund.org

Support Avatar Adi Da's Work
and the Way of Adidam

■ If you are moved to serve Avatar Adi Da's Spiritual Work specifically through advocacy and/or financial patronage, please contact:

Advocacy
12180 Ridge Road
Middletown, CA 95461
phone: (707) 928-5267
email: adidam_advocacy@adidam.org

Order other books and recordings by and about Avatar Adi Da Samraj

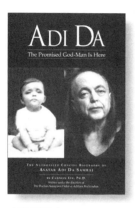

ADI DA

The Promised God-Man Is Here

The biography of Avatar Adi Da from His Birth to present time. Includes a wealth of quotations from His Writings and Talks, as well as stories told by His devotees. 358 pp., **$16.95**

ADIDAM

The True World-Religion Given by the Promised God-Man, Adi Da Samraj

A direct and simple summary of the fundamental aspects of the Way of Adidam. 196 pp., **$16.95**

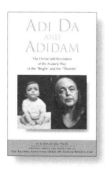

ADI DA AND ADIDAM

The Divine Self-Revelation of the Avataric Way of the "Bright" and the "Thumbs"

A brief introduction to Avatar Adi Da Samraj and His Unique Spiritual Revelation of the Way of Adidam. 64 pp., **$3.95**

THE KNEE OF LISTENING

*The Divine Ordeal Of
The Avataric Incarnation
Of Conscious Light*

*The Spiritual Autobiography
Of The Ruchira Avatar,
Adi Da Samraj*

Born in 1939 on Long Island, New York, Adi Da Samraj describes His earliest life as an existence of constant and unmitigated Spiritual "Brightness". His observation, still in infancy, that others did not live in this manner led Him to undertake an awesome quest—to discover why human beings suffer and how they can transcend that suffering. His quest led Him to a confrontation with the bleak despair of post-industrial Godlessness, to a minute examination of the workings of subjective awareness, to discipleship in a lineage of profound Yogis, to a period of intense Christian mysticism, and finally to a Re-Awakening to the perfect state of "Brightness" He had known at birth.

In *The Knee Of Listening,* Avatar Adi Da also reveals His own direct awareness of His "deeper-personality vehicles"—the beings whose lives were the direct antecedents (or the "pre-history") of His present human lifetime—the great nineteenth-century Indian Realizers Sri Ramakrishna and Swami Vivekananda. Finally, Avatar Adi Da describes the series of profound transformational events that took place in the decades after His Divine Re-Awakening—each one a form of "Yogic death" for which there is no recorded precedent.

Altogether, *The Knee Of Listening* is the unparalleled history of how the Divine Conscious Light has Incarnated in human form, in order to grant everyone the possibility of Ultimate Divine Liberation, Freedom, and Happiness.

The Knee Of Listening *is without a doubt the most profound Spiritual autobiography of all time.*

—ROGER SAVOIE, PhD
philosopher; translator; author, *La Vipère et le Lion:
La Voie radicale de la Spiritualité*

822 pp., **$24.95**

MY "BRIGHT" WORD

by Adi Da Samraj

New Edition of the Classic Spiritual Discourses originally published as *The Method of the Siddhas*

In these Talks from the early years of His Teaching-Work, Avatar Adi Da Gives extraordinary Instruction on the foundation of True Spiritual life, covering topics such as the primary mechanism by which we are preventing the Realization of Truth, the means to overcome this mechanism, and the true function of the Spiritual Master in relation to the devotee.

In modern language, this volume teaches the ancient all-time trans-egoic truths. It transforms the student by paradox and by example. Consciousness, understanding, and finally the awakened Self are the rewards. What more can anyone want?

—ELMER GREEN, PhD
Director Emeritus, Center for Applied Psychophysiology,
The Menninger Clinic

544 pp., **$24.95**

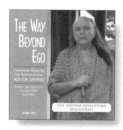

THE WAY BEYOND EGO

Discourses Given by Avatar Adi Da Samraj

The self-contraction, the knot, the action of egoity, must be transcended through recognition-response to That Which Transcends it. This is Given by direct Revelation, and not merely by philosophical propositions. It is not merely to be believed. It must be Revealed.

—AVATAR ADI DA SAMRAJ

In these Talks, Given in 2004 and 2005, Avatar Adi Da elucidates the essence, and the necessary foundation principles, of the Way in His Company. He makes clear that What He is Offering is not a way of self-applied techniques or self-generated experiences—rather, It is a Way of direct relationship to the Divine Person of Love-Bliss, Avatarically Appearing in and as His human Form.

2-CD set
Running times—Disc 1: 71 minutes; Disc 2: 39 minutes
$24.95

New from the Dawn Horse Press—

The Books of the "Perfect Knowledge" Series

The books of the "Perfect Knowledge" Series are drawn from *Is: The Perfect Knowledge of Reality and The "Radical" Way to Realize It,* by the Avataric Great Sage, Adi Da Samraj.

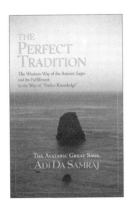 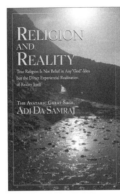 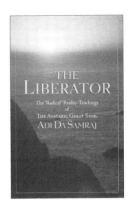

THE PERFECT TRADITION
*The Wisdom-Way of the Ancient Sages
and Its Fulfillment in the Way of "Perfect Knowledge"
by The Avataric Great Sage, Adi Da Samraj*

168 pp., **$12.95**

RELIGION AND REALITY
*True Religion Is Not Belief in Any "God"-Idea but the Direct
Experiential Realization of Reality Itself
by The Avataric Great Sage, Adi Da Samraj*

100 pp., **$9.95**

THE LIBERATOR
*The "Radical" Reality-Teachings
of The Avataric Great Sage, Adi Da Samraj*

160 pp., **$14.95**

The books of the "Perfect Knowledge" Series together comprise the complete text of *Is*.

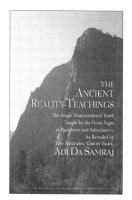 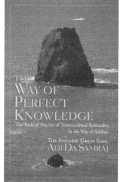 

THE ANCIENT REALITY-TEACHINGS
The Single Transcendental Truth Taught by
the Great Sages of Buddhism and Advaitism—
As Revealed by The Avataric Great Sage, Adi Da Samraj
280 pp., **$19.95**

THE WAY OF PERFECT KNOWLEDGE
The "Radical" Practice of Transcendental Spirituality
in the Way of Adidam
by The Avataric Great Sage, Adi Da Samraj
268 pp., **$19.95**

"RADICAL" DEVOTION
New Writings by The Avataric Great Sage, Adi Da Samraj
A supplement to The Way of Perfect Knowledge
176 pp., **$14.95**

LOVE AND BLESSINGS

The Divine Compassionate Miracles of Avatar Adi Da Samraj

In *Love and Blessings—The Divine Compassionate Miracles of Avatar Adi Da Samraj*, twenty-five of His devotees tell heart-breaking stories of human need and Divine Response. A soldier in Iraq, a woman going blind in Holland, a son with his dying father in Australia, a woman with cancer in America—these and others tell how they asked Adi Da Samraj for His Blessing-Regard and the miraculous process that ensued.

248 pp., **$19.95**

EASY DEATH

Spiritual Wisdom on the Ultimate Transcending of Death and Everything Else
by Adi Da Samraj

This new edition of *Easy Death* is thoroughly revised and updated with:

- New Talks and Essays from Avatar Adi Da on death and ultimate transcendence

- Accounts of profound Events of Yogic Death in Avatar Adi Da's own Life

- Stories of His Blessing in the death transitions of His devotees

. . . an exciting, stimulating, and thought-provoking book that adds immensely to the ever-increasing literature on the phenomena of life and death. But, more important, perhaps, it is a confirmation that a life filled with love instead of fear can lead to ultimately meaningful life and death.

Thank you for this masterpiece.

—ELISABETH KÜBLER-ROSS, MD
author, *On Death and Dying*

544 pp., **$24.95**

The Adidam Revelation Discourses on DVD

In July of 2004, Adi Da Samraj began a series of Discourses that were broadcast live over the Internet to all His devotees around the world. During these remarkable occasions, Adi Da Samraj answered questions from those who were present in the room with Him, but also from devotees in other parts of the world via speakerphone. The "Adidam Revelation Discourse" DVDs offer you the opportunity to see and hear Avatar Adi Da speak in these unique and intimate occasions of Divine Instruction to His devotees. Current available titles include:

TRANSCEND THE SELF-KNOT OF FEAR

Running time: 60 minutes. Includes subtitles in English, Spanish, French, German, Dutch, and Polish.

THE DIVINE IS NOT THE CAUSE

Running time: 72 minutes. Includes subtitles in English, Spanish, French, German, Dutch, Finnish, Polish, Czech, Chinese, Japanese, and Hebrew.

CRACKING THE CODE OF EXPERIENCE

Running time: 86 minutes. Includes subtitles in English, Spanish, German, Dutch, Polish, Czech, Chinese, Japanese, and Hebrew.

DVD, **$26.95** each

To find out about and order other "Source-Texts", books, tapes, CDs, DVDs, and videos by and about Avatar Adi Da, contact your local Adidam regional center, or contact the Dawn Horse Press at:

1-877-770-0772 (from within North America)
1-707-928-6653 (from outside North America)
Or order online from: **www.dawnhorsepress.com**

The Divine Avataric Wisdom-Teaching
of Adi Da Samraj

The Divine Avataric Wisdom-Teaching of Adi Da Samraj is gathered together, in its final form, in the many "Source-Texts" which He has designated as His Eternal Communication to humankind. These "Source-Texts" are "True-Water-Bearers", or Bearers of the "True Water" of the "Bright" Divine Reality Itself.

Avatar Adi Da has grouped His "Source-Texts" into twenty-three "Streams", or "Courses". Each of these Courses conveys a particular aspect of His Divine Avataric Wisdom-Teaching—and each Course (other than the first) may, in principle, include any number of "Source-Texts".

The first Course is Avatar Adi Da's paramount "Source-Text", *The Dawn Horse Testament Of The Ruchira Avatar*. The remaining twenty-two Courses are divided into two groups: *The Heart Of The Adidam Revelation* (consisting of five Courses, which, together, present a comprehensive overview of Avatar Adi Da's entire Wisdom-Teaching) and *The Companions Of The True Dawn Horse* (consisting of seventeen Courses, each of which elaborates on particular topics from *The Dawn Horse Testament*).

> *The "Source-Texts"*
> *(or True-Water-Bearers)*
> *Of My Divine Avataric Wisdom-Teaching*
> *(In Its Twenty-Three Courses Of*
> *True-Water-Born Speech)—*
> *With [My] Divine Testament*
> *As The Epitome*
> *(or First and Principal Text,*
> *and "Bright" True-Water-Mill)*
> *Among Them—*
> *Are, Together, [My] Sufficient Word—*
> *Given, In Summary,*
> *To You*
> *(and, Therefore, To all).*
>
> —Avatar Adi Da Samraj
> *The Dawn Horse Testament*
> *Of The Ruchira Avatar*

The "Source-Texts" of the Divine Avataric Wisdom-Teaching of Adi Da Samraj (in Its Twenty-Three Courses)

The Dawn Horse Testament Of The Ruchira Avatar
(in Its Single Course)

THE DAWN HORSE TESTAMENT OF THE RUCHIRA AVATAR
*The Testament Of Divine Secrets Of The Divine World-Teacher,
Ruchira Avatar Adi Da Samraj*

The Heart Of The Adidam Revelation
(in Its Five Courses)

1. AHAM DA ASMI
(BELOVED, I AM DA)
*The "Late-Time" Avataric Revelation Of The True and Spiritual
Divine Person (The egoless Personal Presence Of Reality and Truth,
Which Is The Only Real Acausal God)*

2. RUCHIRA AVATARA GITA
(THE AVATARIC WAY OF THE DIVINE HEART-MASTER)
*The "Late-Time" Avataric Revelation Of The Great Secret Of The Divinely Self-
Revealed Way That Most Perfectly Realizes The True and Spiritual Divine
Person (The egoless Personal Presence Of Reality and Truth,
Which Is The Only Real Acausal God)*

3. DA LOVE-ANANDA GITA
(THE FREE AVATARIC GIFT OF THE DIVINE LOVE-BLISS)
*The "Late-Time" Avataric Revelation Of The Great Means To Worship and
To Realize The True and Spiritual Divine Person (The egoless Personal Presence
Of Reality and Truth, Which Is The Only Real Acausal God)*

4. HRIDAYA ROSARY
(FOUR THORNS OF HEART-INSTRUCTION)
*The "Late-Time" Avataric Revelation Of The Universally Tangible Divine
Spiritual Body, Which Is The Supreme Agent Of The Great Means To Worship
and To Realize The True and Spiritual Divine Person (The egoless Personal
Presence Of Reality and Truth, Which Is The Only Real Acausal God)*

5. ELEUTHERIOS
(THE ONLY TRUTH THAT SETS THE HEART FREE)
*The "Late-Time" Avataric Revelation Of The "Perfect Practice" Of The Great
Means To Worship and To Realize The True and Spiritual Divine Person
(The egoless Personal Presence Of Reality and Truth, Which Is The Only
Real Acausal God)*

The Companions Of The True Dawn Horse
(in Their Seventeen Courses)

1. REAL (ACAUSAL) GOD IS THE INDIVISIBLE ONENESS OF UNBROKEN LIGHT
   *Reality, Truth, and The "Non-Creator" God In The Universal
   Transcendental Spiritual Way Of Adidam*

   THE TRANSMISSION OF DOUBT
   Transcending Scientific Materialism

2. THE TRULY HUMAN NEW WORLD-CULTURE OF UNBROKEN REAL-GOD-MAN
   *The Eastern Versus The Western Traditional Cultures Of Humankind,
   and The Unique New Non-Dual Culture Of The Universal
   Transcendental Spiritual Way Of Adidam*

   SCIENTIFIC PROOF OF THE EXISTENCE OF GOD WILL SOON BE ANNOUNCED
   BY THE WHITE HOUSE!
   *Prophetic Wisdom about the Myths and Idols of Mass Culture and Popular
   Religious Cultism, the New Priesthood of Scientific and Political Materialism,
   and the Secrets of Enlightenment Hidden in the Human Body*

   NOT-TWO IS PEACE
   The Ordinary People's Way of Global Cooperative Order

3. THE ONLY COMPLETE WAY TO REALIZE THE UNBROKEN LIGHT
   OF REAL (ACAUSAL) GOD
   *An Introductory Overview Of The "Radical" Divine Way Of
   The Universal Transcendental Spiritual Way Of Adidam*

4. THE KNEE OF LISTENING
   *The Divine Ordeal Of The Avataric Incarnation Of Conscious Light—
   The Spiritual Autobiography Of The Avataric Great Sage, Adi Da Samraj*

5. THE DIVINE SIDDHA-METHOD OF THE RUCHIRA AVATAR
   *The Divine Way Of Adidam Is An ego-Transcending Relationship,
   Not An ego-Centric Technique*

   Volume I: MY "BRIGHT" WORD

   Volume II: MY "BRIGHT" SIGHT

   Volume III: MY "BRIGHT" FORM

   Volume IV: MY "BRIGHT" ROOM

6. THE "FIRST ROOM" TRILOGY

    BOOK ONE:
    THE MUMMERY BOOK
    A Parable Of Divine Tragedy, Told By Means Of
    A Self-Illuminated Illustration Of The Totality Of Mind

    BOOK TWO:
    THE SCAPEGOAT BOOK
    The Previously Secret Dialogue on the Avatarically Given Divine Way of
    "Perfect-Knowledge"-Only, Once-Spoken in a Single Night of Conversation,
    Between the Captive Divine Avatar and Great Sage, Raymond Darling,
    and His Captor, the Great Fool, and False Teacher, and Notoriously
    Eccentric Super-Criminal, Evelyn Disk—Herein Fully Given, Without
    Evelyn Disk's Later and Famous and self-Serving Revisions, but Exactly
    As It Was Originally Tape-Recorded, by Evelyn Disk himself, in the First
    Room, at the State Mental Facility, near God's End, and Presented in
    Exact Accordance with the Recent Revelatory and Complete Recounting,
    Given to the Waiting World of Intelligent and Receptive Persons, by
    Meridian Smith, Who Was, As Usual, Inexplicably Present

    BOOK THREE:
    THE HAPPENINE BOOK
    The Childhood Teachings and The End-of-Childhood Revelations of
    The Famous "Infant Sage", Raymond Darling—Compiled from
    Raymond Darling's Original Handwritten Manuscripts, and Privately
    Held Tape-Recordings, Discovered in The First Room By His True
    Servant-Devotee, Meridian Smith, After The Miraculous Disappearance
    of The Divine Avataric Great Sage

7. HE-AND-SHE IS ME
    The Indivisibility Of Consciousness and Light In The Divine Body Of
    The Ruchira Avatar

8. RUCHIRA SHAKTIPAT YOGA
    The Divine (and Not Merely Cosmic) Spiritual Baptism In The Divine Way
    Of Adidam

9. RUCHIRA TANTRA YOGA
    The Physical-Spiritual (and Truly Religious) Method Of Mental, Emotional,
    Sexual, and Whole Bodily Health and Enlightenment In The Divine Way
    Of Adidam

    EASY DEATH
    Spiritual Wisdom on the Ultimate Transcending of Death and Everything Else

    CONSCIOUS EXERCISE AND THE TRANSCENDENTAL SUN
    The Universal ego-Transcending Principle of Love Applied to Exercise and
    the Method of Common Physical Action—A Science of Whole Bodily Wisdom,
    or True Emotion, Intended Most Especially for Those Engaged in Religious
    (and, in Due Course, Spiritual) Life

THE EATING GORILLA COMES IN PEACE
*The Universal ego-Transcending Principle of Love Applied to Diet and
the Regenerative Discipline of True Health*

LOVE OF THE TWO-ARMED FORM
*The Practice of Right Regenerative Sexuality in Ordinary Life, and
the Transcending of Sexuality in True Spiritual Practice*

10. THE SEVEN STAGES OF LIFE
*Transcending The Six Stages Of egoic Life, and Realizing The ego-Transcending
Seventh Stage Of Life, In The Divine Way Of Adidam*

11. THE ALL-COMPLETING AND FINAL DIVINE REVELATION TO HUMANKIND
*A Summary Description Of The Supreme Yoga Of The Seventh Stage Of Life
In The Divine Way Of Adidam*

12. WHAT, WHERE, WHEN, HOW, WHY, AND WHO TO REMEMBER TO BE HAPPY
*A Simple Explanation Of The Divine Way Of Adidam (For Children, and
Everyone Else)*

13. NO SEEKING / MERE BEHOLDING
The Always Primary Practice Of The Divine Way Of Adidam

14. SANTOSHA ADIDAM
The Essential Summary Of The Divine Way Of Adidam

15. THE REALITY-TEACHINGS OF THE SEVENTH WAY

    BOOK ONE:
    UP?
    *Beyond the Beginner's Spiritual Way of Saint Jesus
    and the Traditions of Mystical Cosmic Ascent
    via Spirit-Breath*

    BOOK TWO:
    IS
    *The Perfect Knowledge of Reality
    and The "Radical" Way to Realize It*

    BOOK THREE:
    THE
    Neither Inside Nor Outside Is Reality Itself

THE ALETHEON
The Perfect Summary Of Perfect Truth

16. THE OVERNIGHT REVELATION OF CONSCIOUS LIGHT
The "My House" Discourses On The Indivisible Tantra Of Adidam

17. THE BASKET OF TOLERANCE
The Perfect Guide To Perfectly <u>Unified</u> Understanding Of The One and Great Tradition Of Humankind, and Of The Divine Way Of Adidam As The Perfect <u>Completing</u> Of The One and Great Tradition Of Humankind

NIRVANASARA
The Essence of the Teaching of Reality in the Realistic Traditions of Buddhism, in the Idealistic Traditions of Advaita Vedanta, and in the "Radical" World-Teaching of Adidam

We invite you to find out more about Avatar Adi Da Samraj and the Way of Adidam

■ Find out about our courses, seminars, events, and retreats by calling the regional center nearest you.

AMERICAS
12040 N. Seigler Rd.
Middletown, CA
95461 USA
1-707-928-4936

**THE UNITED
KINGDOM**
uk@adidam.org
0845-330-1008

EUROPE-AFRICA
Annendaalderweg 10
6105 AT Maria Hoop
The Netherlands
31 (0)20 468 1442

PACIFIC-ASIA
12 Seibel Road
Henderson
Auckland 1008
New Zealand
64-9-838-9114

AUSTRALIA
P.O. Box 244
Kew 3101
Victoria
**1800 ADIDAM
(1800-234-326)**

INDIA
F-168 Shree Love-Ananda Marg
Rampath, Shyam Nagar Extn.
Jaipur–302 019, India
91 (141) 2293080

EMAIL: **correspondence@adidam.org**

■ Order books, tapes, CDs, DVDs, and videos by and about Avatar Adi Da Samraj.
1-877-770-0772 (from within North America)
1-707-928-6653 (from outside North America)
order online: **www.dawnhorsepress.com**

■ Visit us online:
www.adidam.org
Explore the online community of Adidam and discover more about Avatar Adi Da and the Way of Adidam.